ADVANCE PRAISE

"The author of *Color My Credit* appears to have done the unthinkable. Not only has Alisa Glutz succeeded in eliminating fear and confusion from understanding and managing our credit, she has managed to make it, dare I say, enjoyable. This book is a gift in that it diminishes the intimidation of one of the greatest hurdles today's homeowner is faced with. Knowledge is power, and now the power is back in the hands of the consumer. Cheers to the author!

~ Todd Newton
Daytime Emmy Award winning television personality
The Celebrity Real Estate Agent® at Newton Luxury Realty

Wow, what a terrific book! So unique, so "colorful!" A whimsical hopeful book about a dark and devastating subject! This read could save family and romantic relationships; a solution to a web of despair with the promise of a happy ending.

~ Susan Sweetow
Realtor Emeritus

"Alisa's ability to take such a complex topic and reduce it into a simple action plan is brilliant! She has spent countless hours investing her heart and soul into this book and I know much good will come from it. It's a must read for anyone who wants to better understand credit."

~ Kelly Zitlow
Vice President CMPS, Certified Instructor ADRE
Cherry Creek Mortgage Company

"Leave it to Alisa to make something as boring as credit full of color and excitement. This book is an easy to follow guide that actually makes credit an approachable subject. The Lord has gifted Alisa to act as a servant leader, filled with joy as she guides the people she helps through the confusion of credit as if sliding down a rainbow. We are blessed to be a part of her journey and this book is a gift."

~ Angela Fazio
Revelation Realty
Designated Broker/Owner
http://bit.ly/ChuckandAngelaFazio

COLOR MY CREDIT

Mastering Your Credit Report — And Score— One Crayon at a Time

Create YOUR Financial Legacy NOW

By

Alisa Glutz

Color My Credit Mastering Your Credit Report —And Score—One Crayon at a Time: Create YOUR Financial Legacy NOW

ISBN-13: 978-0692783528

ISBN-10: 0692783520

Color My Credit also publishes books in a variety of electronic formats. Some content that appears in print may not be available in electronic books. For more information about Color My Credit, LLC, and its products and services contact:

Customer Support
Color My Credit, LLC
4455 E Camelback Road, A-205
Phoenix, AZ 85018

Published in the United States of America

10 9 8 7 6 5 4 3 2 1

DEDICATION

THIS BOOK IS dedicated to my two daughters Angelina Fiona and Brooklyn Isabella, the perfect blend of glitter, fairies, magic, mermaids and all of the wonder in the world. Thank you for bringing me back to your land and reminding me what life was like as a child. Looking through your eyes has helped me find solutions to problems I never would have looking through mine, both in an educational sort of way and a soul sort of way. You have colored my life in so many shades and remind me everyday that miracles happen. May you always keep the sparkles in your eyes and the spirit of wonder in your heart.

TABLE OF CONTENTS

FOREWORD

A WISE MAN once said to me, "Your credit is going to be your best friend, or your worst enemy."

It was true then, and it's true today. In fact, it's probably even *truer* today. The economy is recovering from the worst recession since the Great Depression, interest rates are still at historic lows, and the real estate market is booming. Booming, that is, only for those poised to take advantage of it.

Unfortunately, though, for millions of Americans, what many consider the single greatest step to wealth and financial security—home ownership—is still just a dream. Why? Because of their credit! Either they have bad credit, or no credit at all. And trust me... as a student of all things consumer credit since the mid-nineties, no one knows this more than me.

It all started innocently enough. I was just a dumb kid, fresh out of college, who'd done what so many in college do. I overspent. I did so, largely because of the absence of any real financial education as a youth, and perhaps more so, because of my ever-loosening definition of the word "emergency." The $2,000 in available credit that was in my mailbox the day I arrived at college was a huge gamble on the part of the credit card companies. And it was a gamble they ultimately lost... Big time. But so did I.

I quickly found out the impact of my bad financial behavior, and in turn, the importance of good credit. I couldn't rent an apartment. Opening a checking account was difficult. I couldn't borrow money to buy a car. Heck, I could barely borrow a pen. So I set about the task of exploring my options to repair the damage I'd done. Back then credit restoration wasn't even really a "thing." The only people who did it were attorneys, and they charged a fortune, which, obviously, I couldn't afford. So I read everything I could get my hands on. Legal journals, books, and actual case files at the courthouse were my best sources. Keep in mind, too, this was pre-internet and the process was—*in a word*—exhausting.

Now, over twenty years later, there's quite a bit more information available to the average "dumb kid." Bookstore shelves are loaded with books that promise high scores in no time, and a quick Google search yields literally millions of kits, manuals, and step-by-step guides. There's only one problem; figuring out which of them is worth your time and money, and which of them are garbage. The trick, friends, is figuring out which is which.

So here's a tip from an actual consumer credit expert; ***THE*** consumer credit expert. *(It's true. Google it!)*

*...**You're holding it.***

Color My Credit is the most comprehensive, and innovative consumer credit manual I've seen in a *really*,

really long time, written by one of the most dedicated financial professionals I've ever met.

I first met Alisa Glutz the way many of us meet these days: *Facebook*. I always welcome connections with mortgage and real estate professionals, and she was clearly a very passionate professional in her field. As part of our introduction and initial conversations, I shared some of my consumer credit articles and videos with her. Being the self-proclaimed "credit nerd" that she is it was clear she just couldn't get enough. Not only did she read and watch all of *my* stuff, but every time we talked, she was quick to share with me the latest tip, tool, or technique she'd discovered while reading and watching *other* people's stuff.

As a twenty-plus-year credit nerd myself, I can honestly say that Alisa has the gift (or *curse*) of an insatiable desire for knowledge about all things consumer credit related. She genuinely wants to see people take control of their financial lives, and has created a system so that works brilliantly, using a tool so simple, *even a kindergartner can use it.*

Alisa once shared with me that, as a mortgage professional, knowing how little the average consumer knows about their credit keeps her up at night. Oddly, this book, *the product of so many long hours and sleepless nights*, is her way of educating you, the reader, and in turn, helping *her* rest a little easier. *Color My Credit* is an innovative approach to credit awareness and restoration, which I am confident will be a timeless read, as well as an invitation to connect with and build a long-term relationship with the best in the business!

Doc Compton is a consumer advocate at heart; he works tirelessly to protect consumers' rights, ensuring creditors, collection agencies, and the credit bureaus are held accountable for what they report.

~ Doc Compton
The nation's foremost authority on credit restoration.
http://www.doccompton.com/

ACKNOWLEDGEMENTS

FIRST I HAVE to say this book would have never been developed without my relationship with Jesus Christ. Color is not possible without light. He is the source of my light and I am grateful that he opened my eyes to a beautiful way for me to serve others with the gifts he has given me.

My beautiful ballerinas, Angelina and Brooklyn, supported their mommy every chance they could pointing out anything with crayons or coloring that they saw, memorizing my little parody songs and most of all spending time with me providing inspiration and vision.

Anna Weber—Publisher of Voices in Print and the catalyst in moving this book forward. Thank you for your leadership, education and love. You have more energy than I could ever dream of having. You are solid gold!

Taryl Hansen—My soul sister. Thank you getting what I wanted to do without ever saying a word. You are the best visual interpreter and I am so grateful for your contribution. I value your amazing gifts and most importantly, your friendship.

Peggy Coleman—Mom... my amazingly gifted mother. You inspire me everyday with your passion and expertise in wildlife photography. Thank you for always trusting me enough to give me the freedom to make decisions for myself and always encouraging me to dream big. Thanks for being my mommy and loving me so much. No one could ever replace you.

Heather Wilcox—My sister... you are the only sis I will ever have in the world and I couldn't be luckier. Your humility and strength have inspired me so much in my life and I am so grateful to have that one I can always turn to and know they will be there. Thanks for always keeping me fed.

Ryan Kohls—My warrior brother... you are one of the most unique and beautiful souls I have ever known. Thanks for always loving me and supporting me no matter what. You will always be my baby Ry Ry.

Daniel Harkavy—Owner of the coaching company, Building Champions... for providing a retreat to bring together people who want to live a better life and for teaching me how to develop a plan for my life and my business and for asking the questions most people are too busy to ask, which are more important than anything else.

Bill Hart—Coach with Building Champions... for helping me develop *Color My Credit* from a tiny seed to an actual idea and provide me valuable insight along the way with masterful encouragement and use of your resources.

James Allison—former Coach with Building Champions... for coaching me through and helping me walk out of my darkness. Thank you for your encouragement and unending support.

Kelly Zitlow—My mentor, friend, monkey and "sprinting buddy."

Claxxy Women Club members...thank you for lifting me and supporting me. You are an amazing group of women!

Elisa Lane—Elen Sparks Agency... thanks for believing in this Loan Nut!

Chey Loraine—Thank you for bringing the color out in me. You are the most creative person I know and I will never forget the support you provided me in helping to get Color My Credit off the ground. Smiles!! xo

Tara Kellerhals—My encouraging, lifelong friend. Thank you for pushing me and helping me understand how normal people carry coffee without spilling.

Dreama and Sonny... for always holding the fort and supporting me come hell or high water. You are the greatest team anyone could ever ask for.

Keely Ludick—my soul sister and guardian angel. Thank you for being the Swiss army knife of friends. I'll never leave home without you. You can solve any problem, fix any broken item, sew any dress (or ripped mermaid tail), kill any bug and most of all, love someone who wasn't always worth loving. You walked alongside me during a very dark time. Thanks for being everything you are

My friends and big supporters... who dealt with my countless hours of credit talk or were willing to promote me and support me: Roxanne Auten, Christi Rogers, Gina Chavez, Matt and Keely Ludick, Corey James Wesley, Ross Flurry, Christin Dockery, Brian Pietz, Maverick Commins, Bob Tarics, Larry Bettag, Jami Tadda, Karen Hunt, and Matt Mendonsa.

Steve Scanlon, Bryan Johnson, Noel Villalobos, Parisa Rad, Tisha Marie Pelletier Nikki Stevens, Matt LeDoux, Francisco Aguirre, Carey Pena, Chuck and Angela Fazio, Elena Thornton, David Moskowitz, Laura Holka, Debbie Keller, Nicole Carty, Will Adams, Adam Friedlander, John Ianetta, Karen Wilkens, Ricky Kalmon, Nicole Garcia and Jacqueline Church.

Dea Hutchison, David and Rita Smith, Kyle and Emily Ousley, Krista Ousley, Kacey Ousley, Kody Ousley, Salwa Ebrihim, Todd Newton, Michael Gallagher, Iestyn Dulais, Charlotte Burr, Todd Duncan, Linda Davidson, Dave Savage, Taras Collum, Steve and Judi Marmel, Sondra Burwick, Dave Glutz and Birdie (deceased).

For all those un-named, but residing in my heart and from a place of gratitude for how you show up in my life.

PREFACE

SOMEONE ONCE SAID to me in the early stages of *Color my Credit* being created that it would be "my undoing." Little did I know, that was exactly what I needed—undoing. Unlearning many things I thought were truth. It is definitely a labor of love after being in the mortgage business for 14 years and watching far too many people lose their homes. I have never heard anyone say they learned the fundamentals of building a financial legacy in high school or college or from their parents and still nothing is being implemented. And who wants more math in school? Not me. Mom and dad definitely don't want to deal with the questions their kids will come home and ask following a class on credit scores. Who wants to look like a dummy in front of your kids? Parents can barely handle explaining 4th grade common core. I am passionate about showing people they are smarter than they think and if they learn this legacy piece of life themselves—no one can take that away, and they will have something to pass on one day. I am the anti-credit repair.

You may be wondering what all this creativity and color is about. After all, we are talking about a really serious life issue here: credit! Perhaps you can better understand if you look at being prepared for something as common as weight loss; there is an emotional process you go through.

If you want to lose weight, the first thing is starting with being mindful of what goes into your mouth. You have to create better habits to keep the weight loss under control and research shows it takes 30 days for something to become a habit. Or is it 45 days? I suppose it doesn't matter when most Americans want to know, "How do we get past day four? What's going to keep us motivated along the way?"

We gravitate towards activities that feed our basic needs. Tony Robbins says these six basic needs include:

- √ Certainty,
- √ Uncertainty,
- √ Growth,
- √ Connection/Love,
- √ Significance and
- √ Contribution.

Any three needs being met in an activity will ultimately make it an addiction, good or bad. So what needs are met when looking at our money?

I guess certainty and uncertainty can both be seen in a positive light but most people probably prefer to have their need for uncertainty fulfilled elsewhere. If we want to build a financial legacy we have to find ways to have our basic human needs met by the daily activities required to build wealth so those activities can become habits in our daily life. It's more than just "cutting up credit cards." It's about learning the proper way to use credit cards and implementing better habits; learning with the goal of teaching it to our kids, family and friends. When we learn things with a goal to teach it, we learn it differently.

This is about your legacy... your significance... your contribution. When you enter a mindful zone, it is not about your capacity to learn; it is about your willingness to do so. When you have the materials ready, and easy to access, it is possible to maintain the focus and concentration you need.

You don't need credit repair you need credit education so you can take care of yourself.

It's easier than everyone thinks and it is not necessary

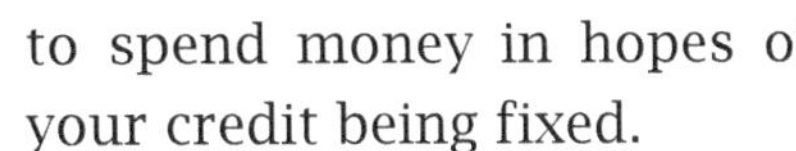

to spend money in hopes of your credit being fixed.

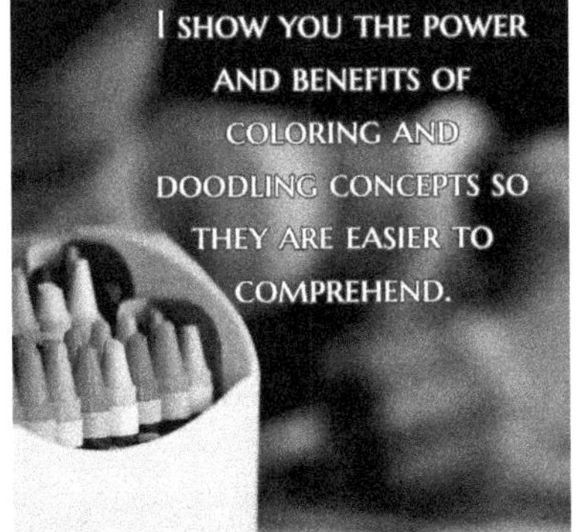

There is **NO** question... credit is an extremely boring subject. By using nostalgic tactics and bringing you back to kindergarten where you first began to learn...

Let's face it... **math** is a favorite subject for few. For most it is a foreign language. What do you do when you don't know a language? You get an **interpreter**!

Money is a universal foreign language for 90% of the world, but 70% of the world are visual learners. While there are seven different areas I believe are key to building a financial legacy, each one includes complicated, overwhelming financial documents that no one understands. My method is to add a little color to the process of learning and help illuminate the most important information on which to focus.

I start with the credit report, which contains 7 to 10 years of information, and can result in a 120 or 150-page credit report.

Who wants to read that?

I first teach you to look for information and color it according to what you see, and then give you an action based on that color. The first thing we do is **THE BLACK OUT** where we black out 70 to 80% of the information that isn't important and has no bearing on the very credit score that is being used to determine how much you will be charged to borrow money or obtain insurance. It's almost like those Magic Eye pictures from the 90s where you stared at them until your eyes could see the picture underneath all the noise. That is all I am trying to do. Cut out the noise and get to what's important for you to focus on and what will have the fastest and greatest impact on your credit score.

When you become a parent, you become a teacher. You have a responsibility to learn the things you never were taught so that your kids have a roadmap to how they will have the best chance at being financially successful in their life. It starts with you. If you don't have kids, you still have a huge part in educating your family and friends and others around you.

What impact are you having on the ones you love?

Just by taking a stand and prioritizing good financial habits, you will inspire those around you to start changing their life, too. You never know who is watching you and hoping to be inspired.

We have to look at credit cards in an entirely new way. Somewhere along the way they created the ability to buy a better life for everyone; a life no one could afford, which was not the purpose. The Great Recession reversed the growth of credit card debt—at least for a few years. According to Transunion, between the first quarters of 2008 and 2014, average credit card debt per borrower fell from a high of $6,276 in mid-2008 to $5,164 in Q1 of 2014—the lowest point in the six-year period.[8] Balances have been creeping up since then at a national level, though some states have seen decreases. In 2015, total outstanding U.S revolving credit card debt was at 937.9 Billion.

Credit card debt fell only after the great recession because **no one was approved for credit cards.**

And minimal education was available on how to re-establish credit and start again. We all still carry a lot of shame about the financial "fallout" and even though many have fought their way back to financial stability, our pride does not allow us to raise our hand and ask the questions that will help us start again.

So we have an opportunity for **a DO OVER**.

As long as we know the right questions to ask...

Credit cards aren't cash and they aren't income. Learn how to use them and then SHARE that with your kids.

Develop better financial habits that they can observe and connect with and build into their own life. Show them you are willing to be brave and vulnerable to better your life. Decide to rise and bring the ones you love along with you.

When one teaches, two learn.

There is no black and white timeline for the impending doom we face if we don't change our financial plan; however, all around us we find the forewarning—foreshadowing of the events that do not color a pretty economic picture for our country or its people. But there's hope. Bob Goff says "God uses kids to remind us of the power of hope in our lives." We have an opportunity as a country to rise from the ashes of the housing crisis and take back our money by connecting with the child in us and approaching our world through their eyes.

Approaching our financial future the way we first learned in life… creating the picture we wanted to see. I am passionate to participate to create a *different legacy* for us all; a colorful, rich legacy that no one can take away.

As a home mortgage professional for 14 years, not only have I had the honor and privilege to transform lives, I have learned the success of approaching something as overwhelming and confusing as credit reports from a child's perspective! You were always curious and asking questions. Let's have some fun with this, shall we?

Remember when you were a kid…

- √ **Remember** fighting tirelessly for something? You just never gave up… you were developing persistence and tenacity.
- √ **Remember** art class! You used colors and creativity… and you learned and actually remembered the information.
- √ **Remember** in sports for you to be successful, you had to learn the rules of the game.
- √ As much as our teachers hated it, we would pass the time in school doodling and allowing the creative right brain to take over. This was where inspiration was born.

Remember, too…

Happiness lies in the joy of achievement, and the thrill of creative effort.

~**Franklin D. Roosevelt** (1882-1945)
American statesman and political leader.

Notice the little things...

It's the little details that are vital. Little things make big things happen.

~ ***John Wooden*** (1910-2010)
Author and American Coach.

Scars are our badges of honor...

One hour of life, crowded to the full with glorious action, and filled with noble risks,
is worth whole years of those mean observances of paltry decorum, in which men steal through existence, like sluggish waters through a marsh,
without either honor or observation.

~ ***Walter Scott*** (1771-1832)
Scottish Novelist

When a child breaks a bone, everyone they know will sign the cast. They become the superstar of the class; the survivor. If a child falls down and cuts itself—everyone around them wants to see the scar; they wear it proudly. Unfortunately, as we get older, we hide our scars; our wounds become our *secrets.* No one wants to be seen as weak or be pitied, so we tell no one when or where it hurts. What children recognize is that scars aren't signs of weakness—a scar is a sign of strength and survival; a story to tell of something they were able to overcome.

Now I obviously don't expect you to jump on your table and let out with a roar "I had a foreclosure" but I do want you to not feel shame for what you might have experienced over the last 10 years. Everyone has a chapter in their story they don't really want to share. The sooner you realize that, the sooner you will be on your way to creating the life you want and using your pain for purpose by learning and then teaching what you know.

No matter where you are starting from, remember... the expert in anything was once a beginner!

The secret of getting ahead is getting started!

Mark Twain (1835-1910)
American writer, entrepreneur, publisher and lecturer.

Before we move forward, let me just share the foundation of my passion with you. People are coming to a point where they want to make changes to their own credit, rather than paying other services for empty promises. The **movement** that is at the heart of my passion for credit restoration reminds me much of the thoughts of Robert Fulghum, who is noted to have said, "Maybe we should develop a Crayola bomb as our next secret weapon."

Is launching this happiness weapon and beauty bomb he suggests the answer to our current financial crisis? Are you inspired to join me in this movement toward self-reliance?

INTRODUCTION

Understanding your credit report and score...
one crayon at a time.

DO YOU REMEMBER the first time you *learned* something in school?

For me, it was how to color! I remember clearly how Mrs. Kirkpatrick would explain, "You must first outline the thing you want to color and then shade it in from there. Otherwise, you will be working without boundaries; you will color outside the lines, and that's not pretty."

So, that was that! That was how you colored, and ultimately, how I learned to set important boundaries.

Unfortunately, when we graduate from high school, we are thrown into a *money world* where there is no Mrs. Kirkpatrick to teach us the rules of the game; how to make it pretty. We go around coloring outside the lines because we don't set right boundaries, and really... we don't even know the benefits of them.

We get jobs, cars and housing and start receiving piles and piles of paperwork, which no one reads and even fewer understand.

Less than favorable actions and beliefs about money and credit have been handed down from generation to generation before the first one of those pieces of financial paperwork is ever received.

I firmly believe we all would *prefer* building a financial legacy... one of which we can be proud and experience the rewards that accompany it. Before that is possible, however, it is essential to understand the inner workings of personal finances, such as how to budget, and how to understand your credit report, taxes, insurance, mortgage and real estate documents, as well having a keen awareness of retirement and legacy documents such as wills and trusts. Color My Credit, LLC. Is a financial education and training company, using the *Color My Method*™ for teaching others how to understand complicated, overwhelming financial documents in a simple, fun and colorful way. Our goal is to jumpstart, or shift thinking about money and other essential financial considerations.

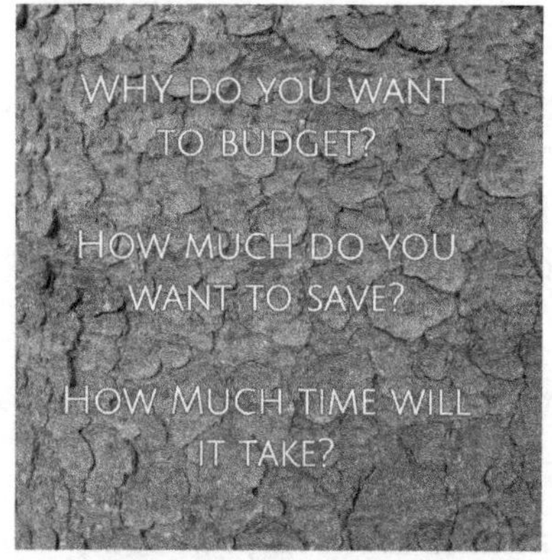

We want people to feel empowered by increasing their financial awareness and

increasing their control in building a financial legacy.

Let me ask you a few rather personal questions...

- √ What do you want from the future, and how are you going to make that happen?
- √ How do you feel about budgeting?
- √ Do you have any debt?
- √ Have you set aside money in savings?
- √ How do you imagine your finances working out best?
- √ Do you believe you are building a financial legacy and impacting the world around you?

Throughout *Color My Credit,* you will discover...

- √ What actions impact your credit score the greatest.
- √ How to go from denial to approval for a car or home loan
- √ How to avoid paying three times the amount of insurance as someone who just got a DUI
- √ What credit bureaus, counseling groups, attorneys and credit repair companies don't want you to know.
- √ How to spot errors and focus on the ones that will have the most positive impact
- √ Discover the pitfalls and things you must avoid (even though they logically seem like they would raise the score) so you don't drop your credit score.
- √ The three key laws you need to understand that will save you thousands over your lifetime
- √ The credit card tricks they don't want you to know that could raise your credit score 100 points or more

√ The REAL way to use a credit card and teach your children about credit cards. Forget everything you know.

Let's start with your Credit Report!

I can promise you, if you can learn how to color, you can learn how to improve your credit score and worthiness.

Welcome to a colorful world of discovering many things, but one of the most important includes a real-life look at how your report is "colored by number!"

Color My Credit

You will have fun, fun, fun as you learn about credit and other financial considerations with simple tools, like the crossword puzzle that follows!

DOWN

1 Allowing the holder to transfer money to another bank account when making a purchase.

2 A plastic card issued by a bank or business for a purchase on credit.

3 The lowest amount able to pay when paying of debt.

5 A person other than the borrower who signs for a loan.

9 Something that is owed or due.

ACROSS

2 The ability to obtain goods or services before payment.
4 Is any fee representing the cost of credit.
5 The amount of credit that a financial institution extends
6 The price paid to a business or bank for borrowing mone
7 An amount paid before it is earned.
8 A record of persons past borrowing and repaying.
9 A way to pay off your debt.

If you remember how much fun you had with dot-to-dots, learning your numbers, shapes and colors in kindergarten, you will love what transpires as your re-fresh and free your mind to playfully learn new skills… credit and financial legacies.

The Credit Dragon…

Section I

KIDS AGAIN...

DO YOU RECALL those first days of school; you were most likely in a constant state of wonder as you learned the proverbial three R's—readin', riten' and 'rithmatic. Once you had mastered those basics, your skills were in a constant state of improvement as learning about the world around you was broken down into subjects such as :

- √ **History**
- √ **Math**
- √ **Art**
- √ **Physical Education**
- √ **English**

And you had action tasks that were expected such as:

- √ **Completing your homework**
- √ **Exploring the Library**

√ **Listening at Story time**

√ **Playing games and puzzles**

Let's start by going back to **Kindergarten** and exploring credit through these subjects and apply some of the actions to help us comprehend and entertain us at the same time. I don't know about you but just holding a crayon is nostalgic for me and instantly brings me back to a time where things were simple.

Coloring is an act of mindfulness that quiets your chattering thoughts and eases your mind. It is an activity that allows you to slow down and be present and in the moment. It can help you lower stress and make you more creative at problem solving. What better mindset to prepare yourself for beginning the exploration of an often-stressful activity like looking at your credit report. Break out your crayons now and just practice doodling below. Just practice and let your imagination create whatever you want. There is no right or wrong. Just create something.

HISTORY CLASS

History, despite its wrenching pain, cannot be unlived, but if faced with courage, need not be lived again.

~ **Maya Angelou** (1928-2014)
American Poet.

History of the Credit Score

APPLYING INFORMATION ABOUT a person to a method that results in the amount being charged started in the early 1800's. When the farmer needed seeds for the harvest, he would go to the general store and promise the store owner that if he could borrow seeds now after the harvest he would come back to pay his bill. This was a great solution for most farmers until Earl showed up. Earl's harvest never happened and he didn't have the money to pay back the storeowner. Soon all over town, word spread that Earl didn't pay his debts and pretty soon Earl wasn't able to support his family.

As the years passed and into the 1900's, oil companies and retail stores offered something similar to the idea of credit today but it wasn't until 1950 when the first credit card came along, Diner's Club. The idea was that people who wanted to lunch now, pay later were given a special card. They could use the card at a string of restaurants that then would invoice you for the amount due once a month. By the end of 1951, there were over 20,000 cardholders.

Just a few years later in 1956, friends Bill Fair and Earl Isaac established Fair Isaac Corporation to develop and market their credit-scoring concept. Initially located in a small apartment in San Rafael, California, Fair Isaac has grown into a NYSE traded company with annual revenues in excess of 600 million dollars. Their credit-scoring model is known as FICO. It wasn't until 1989, as businesses were discovering the power of computerization, Fair Isaac introduced an automated credit scoring software package that was quickly embraced by credit card issuers. But the big catalyst for the near universal acceptance of credit scoring came in 1995 when mortgage giants Fannie Mae and Freddie Mac stipulated that mortgage lenders incorporate FICO scores in their approval process.

Most mortgage lenders require a 620 and potentially go as low as 580 for an FHA loan but in 2007, loan level pricing adjustments were introduced and anyone using credit scores to determine the cost associated with lending you money started calculating charges based on where your credit score fell.

The credit scores, however, weren't always moneymakers for the banks. In fact, in 1978, credit cards weren't doing so well. In the case, *Marquette National Bank of Minneapolis vs- First of Omaha Service Corp*, there was a unanimous decision to allow banks to export credit card rates to states with strict regulations. Banks were borrowing money at higher rates than they could lend (70's inflation high) so the banks moved to non-usury law states (no cap on interest rates charged); interest rates went through the roof and the credit card industry exploded

In 2003, the Fair and Accurate Credit Transactions Act was passed allowing people to have access to their credit report but in 2003, mortgage originations went through the roof and many new loan programs were introduced not requiring more than a pulse to qualify for a home. No one cared about raising your credit score. As the housing market crashed in 2008/2009, credit reports were destroyed and as Americans began to be late on payments, universal default kicked in a domino affect occurred sending consumers into default. In fact, most swore off credit cards as Dave Ramsey's Financial Peace University grew in popularity. Ramsey told consumers, "You don't need credit or a credit score; cut up your credit cards."

The height of the foreclosures and first late payments being made on credit cards occurred around the end of 2009 information stays on your credit report for 7 years from the first late so if you add 7 years to 2009… you get the end of 2016. Now!

When most people hear the words credit history, it sounds like a lengthy review of how you have paid your bills over your lifetime, but credit history really only includes the last 7 years of information (up to 10 in some cases like bankruptcy). Your score is mostly affected by the information reported within the last 24 months. In the timeline chart below, fill in the major events that occurred in your life going back seven years. This will help you in preparing to review your credit. If you have had myriad events in the past seven years, you might want to consider grabbing one of those inexpensive journals and adding these events to your credit journal!

Personal Credit Timeline

Current Year	
1 year ago	
2 years ago	
3 years ago	
4 years ago	
5 years ago	
6 years ago	
7 years ago	

The Chart that follows is a rather lengthy timeline of credit history, beginning in the late 1800's. I don't know how much you enjoyed history class, but I think you might find this particular topic rather fascinating—and what national events drove the changes.

1800's	Country store, credit coins, charge plates	
1900's	Birth of credit though oil companies and department stores.	
1950	Diner's Club: 20,000 cardholders by 1951	
1956	Bill Fair and Earl Isaac create Fair Isaac Company (FICO)	
	1986	FICO went public on the NYSE
	1989	Started selling 1st General Use Credit Score
1958	American Express Diner's card —Run for the money	
		Purple charge card; travel and expenses
		First card made of plastic—replaced cardboard or celluloid
		1 million cards issued, serving 85,000 establishments within first 5 years
		Diners and AMEX
		Closed loop system—in 1986 AMEX became *open*
		Direct merchants Charge for the month; paid in full each month
1966	Birth of revolving debt and general purpose credit cards	
		BankAmerica Card—today known as Visa (1976)
		MasterCard-Interbank—end of closed loop system
		Now, if banks want to issue a credit card, they sign up with Visa or MasterCard Association made up of a board of high-level executives at banks, but are not issued directly from the bank

1970	Credit Card Mania	
		100 million credit cards (not application); "drops" before outlawed
		Fair Credit Reporting Act legislated
1978	Marquette National Bank of Minneapolis vs- First of Omaha Service Corp	
		Unanimous decision to allow banks to export credit card rates to states with strict regulations
		Banks borrowing money at higher rates than they could lend (70's inflation high)
		Big banks move to non-usury law states; interest rates go through the roof
1995	Fannie Mae and Freddie Mac first start using credit scores	
2002	FICO hires Suze Orman as spokesperson and she sells *My FICO Kit*	
2003	Fair and Accurate Credit Transactions Act	
	Allows consumers to view their personal credit reports	
2004	79% of consumer credit reports list at least one error	
2006	Vantagescore is born.	
2007	Loan Level Pricing Adjustments issued by Fannie Mae	
2008	FICO 08 is developed.	
2009	Obama signs into law the Credit Law of '09, which key provisions include:	
	1	Giving consumers sufficient time to pay their bills. Credit card companies have to give consumers at least 21 days to pay from the time the bill is paid. Credit card companies cannot "trap" consumers by setting payment deadlines on the weekend or in the middle of the day, or changing payment deadlines each month.

	2	No retroactive rate increases. Credit card companies must give consumers at least a 45-day notice if the rate is to be increased, and cannot change any terms of the contract within a year. Low introductory rates must extend at least 6-months.
	3	Easier to pay down debt; credit card companies must apply payments to a consumer's highest interest rate balances first. Statements must show consumers how long it would take to pay off the existing balance if the consumer made only the minimum payment, and must show the payment amount and total interest cost to pay off the entire balance in 36 months.
	4	Eliminates the "fee harvester cards." The act restricts fees on low-balance cards sold to cardholders with bad credit. For many of these cards, the up-front fees charged exceeded the remaining credit. The act also restricts the fees that can be charged for gift cards and other prepaid cards.
	5	Eliminates excessive marketing to young people. Consumers under the age of 21 must prove that they have an independent income or can get a co-signor before applying for a credit card. The Act also prevents credit card companies from mailing offers to consumers under 21 unless they "opt-in" and prohibits companies from wooing students with T-shirts, free pizza and other free gifts at university sponsored events.
2009-2010	4th quarter of 2009 – 2nd quarter of 2010 the charge-off rate went from 3% to an unprecedented 10%+	
		Largest drop in American household indebtedness. Charge-offs occur 180 days from first non-payment. Highest 1st date of delinquencies likely '09 summer to beginning of 2010.

Let's talk a little more about timelines; they come into play in many areas that are important to our understanding more than just credit.

In childhood education, learning comes from the teacher's experiences; however, in adult learning, everyone brings to the table their own experience and knowledge which makes the way they learn subjective to their own personal life. As you engage in the Timeline Activity, you will see the value of finding the connecting dots between your experiences and your relationship to credit and money. This is a little different approach than the quick and easy chart previously listed, and may elicit different responses from you.

Create three timelines

1. **Personal timeline** ages 0-10: Identify with your first impressions of money... your first contact with money, first negative money milestone, first positive money milestone, and who was your primary money mentor?
2. **Timeline of last 10 years**: The amount of time information is reported as you take a stroll down memory lane; prepare your mind to look at your credit report and connect it with the last 10 years of your personal life and experiences.
3. **Timeline of next seven years:** As you look forward, keep in mind no matter what your past has looked like, your future is a blank canvas. What goals do you have to which you can apply actionable steps to over the next seven years?

Over the years, helping people with mortgages I have noticed the frustration and anger behind trying to comprehend complicated documents and how it is influenced by the level of anxiety and lack of certainty they have surrounding the topic of money. As you connect with your mindful approach to money, consider whether you ever find yourself saying:

√ I want to buy a home

- √ I want to save money
- √ I want to have an 800 credit score
- √ I want to protect my family from catastrophe
- √ I want to save for retirement
- √ I don't want to pay too much in taxes
- √ I want to leave something behind to my family and or the world

Don't let this wish list frustrate or disappoint you. Just remember the adage about **how you eat a whole elephant... bite by bite.** You must break down each one of your goals into actionable steps to follow and work with professionals who will help illuminate the documents they have made a living in life reviewing. Albert Einstein said "If you can't explain it to a six year old, you don't understand it yourself." Look for financial professionals that are educators at heart and find value in the contribution they make to future generations rather than valuing the contribution you make to **their** lifestyle.

Let's say it is a new school year. You have a brand new teacher. You don't know much about your teacher but what you have heard is that she **often** makes mistakes grading papers. In fact, 79% of the homework assignments she grades have errors. Unless **you** pay attention and catch where she was wrong, you fail the class and have to repeat the year. But that's not fair right? How could a teacher get away with that? What principal would allow her to continue working there?

The problem is she teaches a very complex subject that no one else is capable of teaching as well. The questions she asks are not clear and so there is often a miscommunication between her and her students, which prevents her from giving an accurate grade. Others have tried to do what she can do but none have succeeded. She is an excellent teacher but she is very busy (selling your assignments to other teachers) and relies on her students to pay attention to their work or pay the consequences of **her** errors.

The relationship between you and the credit bureaus isn't that much different. The credit bureaus receive information and give you a grade based on that information. It could be right. It could be wrong. Unless you pay attention, you could be graded on inaccurate information and potentially receive a failing grade (pay thousands of dollars in interest and premiums over your lifetime).

Why color and coloring books... and what's really the connection between color and credit?

It is all about creativity, and using it in a way that transforms thought patterns, increases adaptability and offers myriad other benefits. It is the same reason why adult coloring books are one of the most popular publications being produced today. If you look at those benefits, you will come closer to understanding the foundation behind the *Color My Credit* Method.

The few things that adult coloring books provide an individuals lifestyle may surprise you. Let's take a look at what adult coloring books offer us.

√ They help an individual focus on the actual act of coloring rather than other possible troubling thoughts.

√ They help with emotional stress.

√ Adult coloring books offer adults a way to lessen stress because the distraction.

√ It's been proven to help PTSD, anxiety and even sleep issues.

√ Memories, it brings us back to a time and helps us reminisce (which can be healthy).

√ The brain actually enjoys when people color (seriously) it utilizes an area of the brain that will enhance focus and concentration.

√ It helps with problem solving and organization.

Did you know... coloring uses both sides of the brain?

The right and the left side of the brain, which is really good, because **we need and benefit from both**.

Three Credit Bureaus Fact Cheat Sheet

WHEN YOU OPEN a new account, the information is often reported to the three credit bureaus. Companies extending credit are not *required* to report and sometimes only report to one or two of the bureaus. This is partly why we see such a variation in the scores. Credit accounts are not required to report to the three credit bureaus, they are just required to report accurate and verifiable information if they do report it. Each of the three has specific names for the models used depending on the industry or type of creditor who pulls the credit report. To make a point; if you go to www.myfico.com, if you were to purchase 19 credit scores at this time for a fee, you could see the variation of your score depending on who pulled your credit.

SO again just to make it clear:

You open an account with a company and the account-holder then reports your information once a month to one or all three of the credit bureaus—Transunion, Equifax and Experian—and the credit bureaus use the FICO scoring model required to be used for that specific institution to calculate a score for you.

You don't have disputes with FICO; they are nothing more than a robot. What you must dispute and know is the information going into the robot—or I should say the three robots.

Robots are probably the best way to describe the three bureaus and their disputing process in our country. All disputes are automated where there is no live person reading the information and reviewing the records. Plans are in place to change that but little has been done.

Review the cheat sheet below, provided to to help you understand the distinctions between the three companies and then challenge yourself in the Credit Bureau Match Up.

The following includes highlights of the differences between each credit bureau's reports—and how that information can help you to both better understand and improve your credit rating.

Equifax Highlights

As of this writing, Equifax reports are the only ones that summarize "Open Accounts" and "Closed Accounts," making it far easier to distinguish this information and choose which accounts you want to examine first. (With Experian and TransUnion, all accounts are grouped together and listed alphabetically).

Equifax files also often show an 81-month credit history for your credit accounts. In some cases, however, particularly for closed or paid accounts, you will see a statement saying: "No 81-Month Payment Data available for display."

Experian Highlights

Experian shows you "Status Details" indicating when an account is scheduled to fall off your credit report, which is a favorite of the bureau's features.

For example, since positive payment history remains on your credit report for 10 years, an auto loan that you paid off and closed in July 2008 will show the following Status Details: "This account is scheduled to continue on record until July 2018."

By contrast, let's say you had an account go to collections... and ultimately get written off by a creditor. The original first date of delinquency would be used to determine rating and would show the account continuing on record for seven (7) years. This is very helpful in determining how long the debt will haunt you. With Experian credit files, you will also see a monthly "Balance History" for any accounts that are still open, or for those closed accounts with an outstanding balance.

Transunion Highlights

Transunion has the most thorough employment data section in your personal summary. You can update or correct several fields, including: your current or previous employer's name, the position you held, and the date you were hired.

Changing this information will not improve your credit score. However, if you ever seek a loan in the future, it will be helpful to have your information accurately reflected in your credit report to show a lender your hire date for a job, or the length of time you spent at a specific employer

TransUnion reports list both "Satisfactory" and "Unsatisfactory" accounts. They also include color-coded boxes (white, green, yellow, orange and red), with words or numbers inside of them, to indicate your payment history:

√ A white box with an "X" indicates unknown information

√ A green box with "OK" signals that your payment is current.

√ A yellow box with "30" means you were 30 days late on a payment.

√ An orange box with "60" means you were 60 days late.

√ A red box with "90" means you were 90 days late.

√ A red box with "120" means you were 120 days late.

Lastly, TransUnion also uses the notation "N/A" or "Not Applicable" to describe various accounts.

The Information Found In All Credit Reports

ALL CREDIT REPORTS—whether from Experian, Equifax or Transunion—contain basic information that can be categorized into the five primary sections noted as follows:

Personal Information

These personal facts about you include your full name, date of birth, address, place of employment, and a partial listing of your social security number.

Summary of Accounts

Your account summary lists any information creditors have reported about your payment history on loans of all kinds, such as mortgages, auto loans, credit cards and student loans. There are many accounts you might think report to the credit bureaus that you make monthly payments to—but unless you **stop paying them** and they become a collection will never show up on your credit. There are more and more collections showing on credit for cell phones, gym memberships and utilities but none of those types of accounts ever show up as a positive account.

Public Records

Any public record on your credit file—such as a judgment, tax lien or bankruptcy—will seriously lower your FICO credit score. However, judgments or bankruptcies listed as "dismissed" will not impact your credit rating because credit-scoring firms will ignore them, as if they never happened. Public Records are not creditors that report to the credit bureaus. The bureaus hire third party companies to research county recorded documents, which they manually add these accounts to your credit report.

Most of the time judgments are not updated on your credit until you send in the satisfaction of the judgment to each of the three credit agencies to have them update your records. Always be thorough in your follow-up to get the documentation proving your debts have been satisfied. Without proof of payment, you could end up having to pay it again to the next debt buyer who purchases it thinking it is an open collection or judgment on which they can collect.

Inquiries

An inquiry in your credit file is a record of any application for credit that you made.

For example, if you seek a mortgage or car loan, or even if you apply for a credit card or perhaps request an increase in your current credit card limit, any of these actions can result in an inquiry, also known as a "hard" pull of your credit file. (Pulling your own credit report is a "soft" pull and doesn't impact your credit rating).

Consumer Statements

Under the Fair Credit Reporting Act, you are allowed to add a 100-word "Consumer Statement" to any of your credit reports if you have disputed an item in your credit files, but the item was not removed because a creditor verified it.

Scrutinizing your credit reports puts you one step closer to achieving a great credit rating because you will undoubtedly become better educated about your credit just looking at the highlights of each credit file, and the way similar information is presented differently in each credit report.

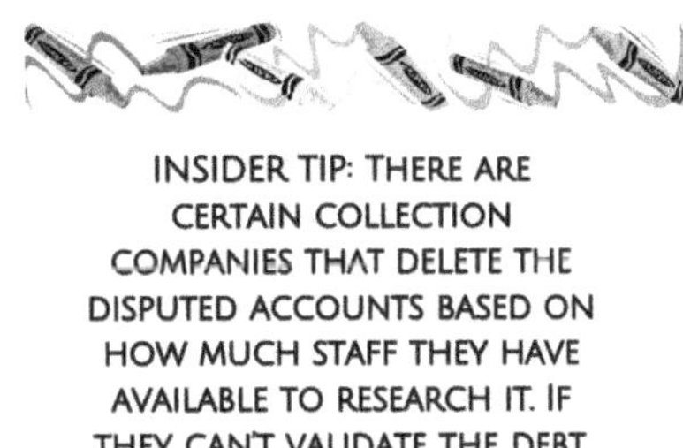

You'll only be able to spot these differences, though, by closely examining your credit reports generated by Equifax, Experian and Transunion.

Three Laws to Memorize

I KNOW, YOU didn't really expect to have to memorize this information, but I promise there won't be a lot of it. In fact, you might want to keep this book really handy so you can refer to it when necessary.

- √ **Fair Credit Reporting Act (FCRA)** – basically tells the credit bureaus what they can and can't do. All Credit Bureau Disputes utilize the FCRA
- √ **Fair Credit Billing Act (FCBA),** which is a subset of the more comprehensive Truth in Lending Act essentially, tells original creditors how they should behave. This law is really effective for disputing debt directly with the original creditor.
- √ **Fair Debt Collections Practices Act (FDCPA)** regulates debt collectors (buyers of debt from original creditors). Best to be used with disputing with collection companies.

Doodle

Color the World a Better Place with Good Credit

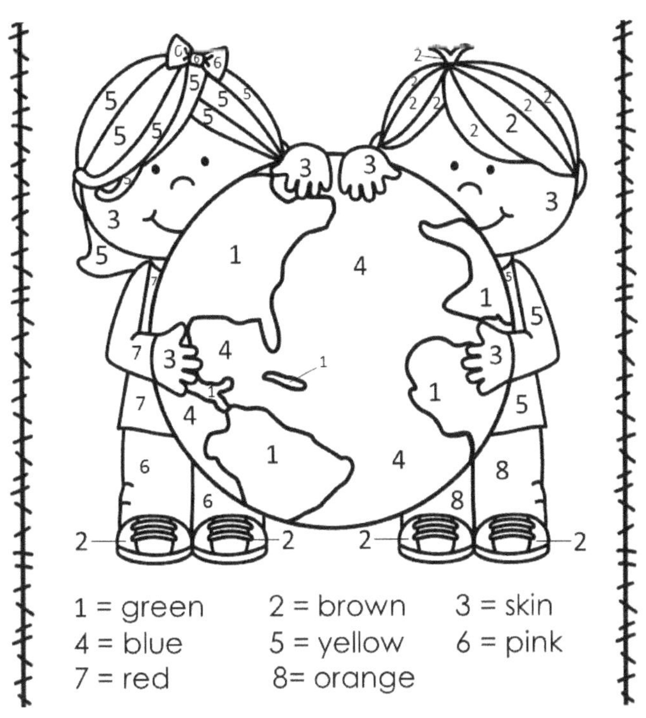

MATH CLASS

Life is a math equation. In order to gain the most, you have to know how to convert the negatives into positives.

~ Unknown

Life is a Math Equation.

I AM QUITE positive none of your teachers went to great lengths to make sure you understood this e secret, magical math of credit scores! Pretty much everyone is aware the higher your credit score, the more favorable financing options you have, but just what goes into those *mystery numbers* just might surprise you. Actually, credit reports are intended for financing entities—not for consumers! They are used as a reliable assessment to tell a potential lender how likely it is that you will follow through on your agreement. Think about this: In any financing agreement, there is money involved; often a great deal of it.

- √ Does it not make sense that lenders want a **score they can trust?**
- √ Does it not make sense that score providers keep their algorithms a secret to **prevent** consumers from manipulating those scores?
- √ If we were able to influence our scores, they'd no longer be an

√ **accurate gauge of risk**
and would be worthless to banks, mortgage companies, and other financing entities. We can, however, trust credit-scoring models to ultimately reward strategic and responsible actions and reflect creditworthiness.

Who Ran my Credit?

Home and Auto Loans

YOU ARE FORTUNATE that credit-scoring systems allow you to shop for the best rates on car loans without having a negative impact on your credit scores. The bureaus do so by counting all inquiries for auto loans within a certain period of time as one single inquiry.

Now, that time period varies slightly from one credit scoring system to another but typically is 14-days, which allows ample time to be approved by your bank or credit union—or car dealerships who frequently shop multiple lenders in a practice commonly known in the industry as shot-gunning to help the customer find the best loan terms.

When you are considering a large purchase such as this, it is best to get a copy of your report in advance of the "shopping" to make sure everything in it is accurate—and alert you to what may need improvement.

I also encourage you to consider purchasing a credit score at least once when you request your personal credit report. The credit score will come with a description of what issues most affected it—both positively and negatively. Those factors are specific to your personal credit report and will enable them to identify the specific steps you need to take to become more credit-worthy.

Credit scores are unique to each individual's credit history, so I don't give off-the-cuff advice... while it might be good advice for one person, it could be damaging for another, which is precisely why I continue to assist with understanding the fullness of your reports to make sure you have "reasonable" expectations, based on your overall fiscal picture, and prevent disappointment when you are actually forced to deal with the facts and what you can or cannot do about modifying them.

Employment

In recent years, more and more employers have begun to check credit reports prior to making hiring decisions. And it is not unheard of for employers to check credit reports on existing employees—demanding they meet certain minimum to remain employed. Given the lack of education in this country and that employers don't receive a credit score—just data—how many of them actually know what they are reading?

Rental Opportunities

Landlords and rental communities check credit as a standard part of their tenant screening process. As this practice has become commonplace, those with credit issues have often found themselves struggling to find acceptable housing.

Insurance Costs

Home and auto insurers, almost without exception, incorporate credit scores in their underwriting and pricing formula. The quality of your credit can make a dramatic difference in your monthly insurance premiums.

Utility Companies and Other Home Services

The inquiries are scored because they are an indication that you may have taken on new financial obligations that could impact your ability to manage additional new debt. Like all inquiries, they have minimal impact on credit scores, and that impact is even less after 3 to 6 months.

You may feel relieved to discover that most *positive payment* of cable, utilities, Internet services and telephone is not reported. Unfortunately, should you fail to make timely payments for these services, you will *discover* the negative information may be reported in the form of a collection account, which is a huge indicator it is to your best benefit to make the payments in full—and as agreed.

In the past positive rent payment was not reported; recently, Experian became the first national reporting bureau to report on-time rent payment history; information that is now available to be included in credit score calculations.

The intent to share the categories in a review of who has run your credit is to give emphasis to the part positive payment history plays. This can be particularly important if you are trying to establish first time credit—or trying to rebuild your credit history following a financial struggle.

How Many Scores Do I Have?

ONE OF THE first things you need to be really familiar with are the three primary reporting bureaus: Experian, Equifax, Transunion—or—as I like to think of them: Burger King, In-and-Out, and McDonalds!

If you want a cheeseburger and order one from each of those restaurants, are you going to get the same cheeseburger? It might have the same ingredients but will it be layered the same way? Will the ketchup and mayonnaise be mixed together in to some special sauce? Will it taste exactly the same? No; neither will the three credit scores the three bureaus look the same.

You would do well to understand these three different reporting companies do not play nice with each other and share your important information, nor are they government-controlled. Even if you provide what the other company is reporting they will not change the report. They did, however, bond together sufficiently to come up with a joint venture to rival FICO scores with a competitor called Vantagescore. Unfortunately Vantagescore didn't quite catch on and less than 3% of all creditors use it... but it sure does a good job creating confusion as the score offered on all the free websites, but not used when buying a home or a car. It looks very similar to a credit score with a similar range but the algorithm—or what the recipe consists of for the score—is completely different from FICO.

What is your FICO score based on?

√ **35%** is weighted towards your payment history and whether you make your payments on time, have any recent collection accounts or public records reporting or had recent activity on a derogatory account on your credit report.

√ **30%** emphasizes the amount you owe on revolving credit, which is compared to the amount of credit you have available. You want to keep this ratio low (between 10-20% ideally) so it appears you use credit wisely and not using it in place of income or as cash.

INSIDER TIP: WHEN YOU MAKE THE LAST PAYMENT ON A CLOSED ACCOUNT, THE ACCOUNT'S LENGTH OF HISTORY IS MOVED OUT OF THE MIX OF YOUR LENGTH OF HISTORY. CLOSING OR PAYING OFF A CLOSED ACCOUNT CAN HAVE A BIG IMPACT ON YOUR CREDIT SCORE.

- √ **15%** measures the length of your credit history. The longer your history the better—which can be difficult to achieve when trying to get your first credit card, or car loan. This percentage also takes into account how often your use your accounts; regular use and repayment show responsible credit use.
- √ You can identify if an account reporting is affecting the length of history by looking specifically at the date opened and the date of last activity on an open account. **10%** accounts for the types of credit you have in use. Responsible use of a mix of credit types, such as a credit card, a gas or retail card, and an installment loan for a car payment shows you understand the different uses for credit.
- √ **10%** assesses how much of your credit is newly opened credit. Someone looking for more credit that is opening many accounts in a short period of time is more likely to be considered a credit risk.

Numbers of Scores and Scoring Models

YOU MIGHT BE surprised to know FICO has developed over 50 different models for each credit agency; depending on the industry and end user. When you take advantage of the pro-offered free FICO score, you will likely get one of the following:

1. The FICO 98-score
2. FICO '04 score (introduced in 2004).
3. FICO '08 score (introduced in 2008).

Fannie Mae and Freddie Mac are very specific in the scoring models they will accept in approving a mortgage, and require what is known as a Tri-merged Credit Report. When the FICO '08 model was introduced, Fannie Mae and Freddie Mac never adopted it; today they still accept only the following:

1. Experian Fair Isaac—Version 2.
2. Transunion Classic '04.
3. Equifax Beacon '05.

Vantage/FICO Algorithms and Differences

Credit scoring **has become** big business! FICO generated $748.22 million dollars in 2014. Some companies make it big while others just don't quite reach that peak, such as VantageScore Solutions (VSS). The company, created in 2006 just never took off despite improvements added in versions 2.0 and 3.0. Let's look at how VantageScore's model differed from FICO.

- √ **32%**—payment history.
- √ **23%**—credit utilization (the amount of credit used/divided by total credit limit available).
- √ **05%**—balances
- √ **13%**—depth of credit
- √ **10%**—recent credit

√ **07%**—available credit

Other key differences include the fact that paid collections, which greatly impact FICO scores... are reflected quite differently with VantageScore, who varies significantly in its timeline before credit is established.

One has to wonder at the equity of banks giving out credit scores, but happen it does!

√ **Wells Fargo** gives out Experian's VantageScore.

√ **PenFed** provides free FICO NextGen scores online.

√ **USAA** provides free Experian VantageScore to members.

√ **US Bank** offers free Experian consumer model credit scores to customers.

√ **Ally** shares free Transunion consumer odes FICO scores.

As I encourage you to head back to math class and figure out your numbers, you will be happy to know there are several websites, which offer your free VantageScore if you allow the company to market your personal information:

√ **CreditKarma**—Transunion/Equifax VantageScores

√ **CreditSesame**—Experian VantageScore

√ **Quizzle**—Experian VantageScore

√ **Credit.com**—Personal version of credit score based on Experian data

In all available credit scores—mortgage scores are not available to consumers.

FAQ

CREDIT SCORES ARE just one of the many topics in life to which you might not know the answers... because you don't know what questions to ask. The following are questions that are frequently brought to me by clients, which I want to share with you—just because **you don't know what you don't know**!

1. John M. asks, "I am really frustrated the credit card company raised my interest rate even though I've always paid my bills on time. What can I do?"

Color My Credit: *John, in the past credit card issuers could raise your rate—at any time, and for any reason. However, with the inception of the Credit Card Act, this activity is no longer allowed. It is allowable to increase rates on outstanding balances when the consumer is more than 60 days late. The rate may also be increased on new purchases, provided you are given 45 days notice, which would give you ample time to cancel the account if you choose.*

In your instance, the best thing is to request a lower rate; if you cannot negotiate that, consider transferring your balance to another card.

2. Melissa R. who had worked hard to clean up here credit was in tears as she asked the following: "A debt collector just contacted me about an old debt, and before I take any action, I want to know... do I have to pay it?"

Color My Credit: *There is no immediate answer to this, Melissa. You see, every state has a statute of limitations governing just how long the creditor or collector has to sue you. If the debt is too old and a collection suit is initiated, you may be able to raise the statute of limitations as a defense. For more specific information, we would need to review the particulars of that debt and check with your state attorney general's office or a local consumer attorney.*

If it is outside the bounds of the statute of limitations, you can contact the collection agency, indicate you believe this is the status, and instruct the company to cease its attempts to collect. Make sure you send the letter by certified mail and retain a copy for your records.

If your greater concern is your credit report, remember collection items can only be reported for up to 7 ½ years from the date you ceased making payments to the original lender—regardless whether they are paid or not.

3. Lance W. was getting all kinds of credit advice from his friends, telling him how many cards he needed to have in his wallet. Not wanting to risk the good credit he had worked hard to establish, Lance inquired, "I don't want to make a mistake here by listening to people who may not really know how all this credit score stuff works, so... what exactly is the ideal number of credit cards I should consider having?"

Color My Credit: *Well, Lance, I think at the end of the day what really matters is what you perceive is ideal! Most people will be just fine with two major credit cards: one that is a low-rate card should you ever need to carry a balance, and the other—a card with a grace period. Unless you plan to use the card heavily to take advantage of the rewards, a card with no annual fee would be best... weighing the cost of the fee against those rewards.*

If the "ideal" number is to improve your credit score, two should be sufficient, although if managed well, more cards will not damage your score. Generally, four credit accounts of varying nature—mortgage, car loan, major credit card and retail card—is the ideal mix of active cards paid monthly.

Caveat: If you currently have a large number of cards ***do not close them*** *hoping it will boost your credit score—closing them may actually cause your score to drop.*

4. Allison S. is a worried mother who is concerned about a son who has gotten in over his head. She called asking, "My son, Daemon, has had some recent financial difficulties that has left him with a lot of debt. What is the best way to help?"

Color My Credit: Honestly, Allison, the best way to help Daemon is to give him some credit literacy materials to help him really learn and understand how to manage his debt. My guess is you are calling because he just asked you for a consolidation loan to help pay off his debt, and although you want to be the supportive parent, you aren't sure if that is the best direction to take. First, I would say to trust your instincts, if you feel Daemon's issue is an inability to manage money, then you may do little more than enable him, rather than learning life's money lessons. Even if he is in deep trouble right now—assuming his responsibility is not like to be a good long-term solution!

If you are highly disinclined to say no, then consider one of these two solutions:

Give Daemon a gift… not a loan. There will be no hard feelings when it is not repaid!

Agree to assist him only if he is willing to an official loan agreement, with an automatic payment to your checking account. You can spread the amount and term out as long as you choose, but he is still learning the lesson of financial responsibility and accountability—each of which is a valuable lesson.

4. Lucille D. was recently widowed. Her husband had always managed their finances and only upon his death did she discover a frightening, looming amount of debt. Her question: "My husband just passed away and left me with more debt than I ever knew could exist, do I have to pay it?"

Color My Credit: First, Lucille, I am extremely sad for your loss, and happy to see what I can do to put give you clarity during what must be a difficult time. In most cases, you are not responsible for another person's debt when they die, unless you are a co-signer on the account. In your case however, and since you do live in one of the community property states (Arizona, California, Idaho, Louisiana, Nevada, New Mexico, Texas, Washington, Wisconsin), debts incurred during your marriage are considered community property and you are likely responsible for them.

When someone passes with outstanding debt, creditors look first to co-signers, and then to the estate. If the amount is relatively small, some creditors don't bother to pursue payment, but there is no guarantee what will transpire in your particular situation.

Not knowing other particulars of your husband's other assets or estate matters, if you are being pressured to pay a debt, which you do feel is equitably yours, you would do well to contact an estate planning or consumer law attorney.

7. Mike G. has found himself up against the proverbial wall and feels he has no recourse but to file a bankruptcy, but... "I don't have the money to file for bankruptcy. I am retired and Social Security is my only source of income, and that barely covers my basic needs. Following a serious health

issue, I found myself over my head in credit card debt and they are hounding me! What can I do?"

Color My Credit: It sounds like you really are up against it Mike, let's see what that looks like when you have little to no income and no assets. This is a valid picture of someone who is considered "judgment proof," and means even if someone tried to sue you for the debt, there would be no way to force you to pay. Fortunately, creditors generally cannot seize your Social Security payments to pay debts—and should you have any retirement accounts, they are normally protected from creditor claims. If these apply to you, there may be no reason for you to even file for bankruptcy.

However, my best professional counsel in this situation is to encourage you to visit with a reputable bankruptcy attorney to thoroughly assess your situation, especially if you do have assets, such as a home or money outside retirement accounts.

If there is no doubt you are judgment proof, you will likely be able to stop the "hounding" by writing them a letter stating you have no income other than Social Security payments and no assets. Explain you have to way to pay, and request they stop contacting you. Send the letter certified mail, and keep copies of your letter and any future mail received from them. If you receive any correspondence they plan to sue you, immediately contact a consumer law attorney.

8. Stephanie L. is a newbie to the credit world! She is interested in learning how to manage her scores so she can plan a financial legacy that will make her parents proud of her. Her concern, "I want to know what I am starting out with, and what I may have to fix. So, will checking my credit report hurt my credit score?"

Color My Credit: You should be really proud of yourself, Stephanie! And I am happy to report when you check your own credit report through a service that sells directly to consumers, it is considered a soft inquiry. They are listed when you review your own report, but are not visible to creditors and do not affect your credit scores. In fact, you can request an annual report from each of the three primary bureaus. It is great that you want to get up close and familiar with your report, so go for it!

9. Robin C., another concerned consumer wanted to know, "Just how much are my scores reduced when I have an inquiry on my credit report?"

Color My Credit: Unfortunately, Robin, this is not an easy answer. There are a lot of moving parts in the algorithms that assess your score. However, in general, inquiries may account for less than 5% of your score so the stronger it is, the less likely an inquiry or two will have a significant impact.

Nonetheless, proceed with great caution when applying for new credit for anything: cell phones, retail cards, insurance, etc. Each will result in a credit check, and if you are in the process of securing a mortgage, just a few points lower on your credit score can represent a large difference in your rate and ultimate payment.

10. Samantha W. has been caught in the throes of a divorce and the credit damage that is all too often a part of the overall experience. While trying to make a new life for herself, she wants to know, "My ex-husband was supposed to pay this account by the terms of the Decree. Now, I am trying to get on with my life and unexpectedly discovered he didn't, and it damaged my score. Now what do I do?"

Color My Credit: I am afraid I don't have wonderful news for you on that, Samantha. Joint accounts just seem to continue to create problems long after the Decree has supposedly settled things. According to the creditor, you are essentially a co-signer on the account, and the agreement in the Decree is between you and your former spouse that was never approved by the creditor. As far as they are concerned, that Decree doesn't erase the original agreement with the lender.

When it comes to your credit score/report, the late payment will be deemed accurate since the account is still yours until it is paid off, closed, or refinanced into your former spouse's name. Some creditors, when provided proof of the Decree will agree to remove the damaging notations from the innocent spouse's credit report, but may require it be paid off first.

Unfortunately, this puts you in the position of contacting your attorney to force your former spouse to honor the terms of the divorce decree.

Doodle...

Let this be your **Yellow Brick Road** and doodle in the path that represents the fun things you can have in your life... once your credit scores are more in your favor. The following is just an example... grab your crayons and have fun!

Write down the feeling you have when you start this doodle, and once you have completed the exercise, skip back and write down how you feel at the finish!

ART CLASS

Art is not what you see, but what you make others see.

~ **Edgar Degas** (1884-1917)
French author and artist.

Where Color Inspires...

WHAT DO YOU think—do art teachers have any difficulty inspiring students and allowing them to be creative and have fun? Do you see credit management as a science? What if I can show you how to transform this pesky task into a fun, and creative, art form? Do you remember how I spoke of my kindergarten teacher teaching about creating the boundaries within which we were to color? For me that made such practical sense and I felt, "That is that! That is how you color!" Well, in mastering the fine art of credit score transformation, you are going to learn how to put a framework in place; a boundary if you will, to color a better, brighter credit score.

If you want to engage with me now, head over to www.annualcreditreport.com and print down your three credit reports.

You see, every 12 months you are entitled to one free copy of your credit reports from each of the three nationwide credit reporting agencies: Experian, Equifax, and Transunion. You can also get a yearly free copy of any specialty consumer reports; in some instances, you can get free reports more than once per year. You must use the above-noted URL to get the raw data for FICO. This is the same site the government sends consumers to for their free annual report.

Don't be deceived by the millions of other sites offering "credit reports!"

Now... get ready for a little enlightenment, color and inspired credit awareness, as you follow through the color-coding process listed as follows. The tools you are going to need include your Credit Report, crayons, a calculator, and a calendar (phone or planner).

BLACK OUT accounts that are:

- √ Closed
- √ Derogatory accounts with a zero balance and have not been reported in the past 24 months.

COLOR GREEN all accounts that are:

- √ Open
- √ Reporting to all three bureaus
- √ Data reported and active within the last 24 months
- √ Balance below 20% of your limit

COLOR RED all accounts that are:

- √ Open
- √ Revolving accounts
- √ Balance showing more than 20% of your limit

COLOR YELLOW all accounts that are:

- √ Open

- √ Revolving
- √ Date of last activity more than six months old

COLOR BLUE all accounts that are:

- √ Deferred accounts
- √ Student loans or notes

COLOR PURPLE all accounts that are:

- √ Derogatory
- √ Any accounts currently showing in dispute

COLOR ORANGE all accounts that:

- √ Needs to be disputed, settled, or corrected

Ok! Admit it—that was a much different approach to looking at this much *credit* information than you previously have. I am sure some of the stress you would normally feel was replaced with the fun of color—and the guidance you were provided to sort it all out and make some sense of it all. Now, we are going to take the next step and really take a deep dive into looking at the report by following the Checklist, which will help you catch any possible errors on the report.

Personal Information

Your credit score does not take into account any personal information. It just identifies who you are but that is important because your report needs to be your information!

People are surprised to see their income, job title and amount in their bank account is not reported on their credit report and has no bearing on their score.

Your credit score doesn't care about your gender, sexual orientation, age or who you are dating. It just wants to know how you compare to others you have been grouped with... according to your fiscal behavior.

Think of it this way: Remember in high school when everyone had a clique they seemed to belong to even if you didn't? Which meant that you belonged to the *no-clique-clique*.

Well, credit scoring is kind of similar. Everyone is grouped in about 10 different cliques (or in the credit industry we call them scorecards). Your behavior is what keeps you in the clique. If you want to be Prom Queen or King, you need act like the other Prom Queens and Kings. The more you act like a particular group, the more you stay in that group. If you rise above and start engaging in better behavior, you will move into a new group and be compared to others in it. Making a bad choice could send you right behind the school cafeteria where the kids who flunked out hang out. Only time and good behavior will get you out of there.

Check Personal Records

Check over the personal records just to make sure you being identified correctly and make notes of any information that should be disputed and corrected.

- √ Incorrect or incomplete name, address or phone number.
- √ Lack of prior address—if you have not resided long at your current one.
- √ Incorrect Social Security Number or birth date.
- √ Incorrect, missing, or outdated employment information.
- √ Incorrect marital status—such as a former spouse listed as your current partner.

Check Public Records

Review the other two main sections besides the closed accounts. Be prepared for this to be a lengthy, but oh so necessary process. Failure to take this step is like one of those old clichés about biting off your nose to spite your face!

Ready, set, go!

- √ Lawsuits in which you were **not** involved.
- √ A bankruptcy filed by a spouse or ex-spouse, even though you personally did not file bankruptcy.
- √ Bankruptcies that you filed more than 10 years ago, or that are not identified by the specific chapter of the bankruptcy code.
- √ Lawsuits or judgments reported more than seven years after judgment was entered, or after the expiration of the statue of limitations.

- √ Tax liens you paid more than seven years ago.
- √ Paid tax, judgment, mechanics, or other liens listed as unpaid.

Credit Accounts

- √ Co-mingled accounts—credit histories for someone with a similar or same name.
- √ Accounts listed as joint when only your spouse is responsible for the account or vice versa.
- √ Premarital debts of your current spouse, attributed to you.
- √ An account due to an identity thief's actions.
- √ Accounts on which you are an authorized user or are not included in the report, which may happen with accounts in one spouse's name, for which the other spouse is authorized for use.
- √ Incorrect account histories—such as a late payment notation when you know you have paid on time.
- √ Failure to list a zero balance for a debt that was discharged in bankruptcy, or showing a discharged debt as still owing.
- √ Failure to show a delinquent debt has been discharged in bankruptcy.
- √ A voluntary surrender of your vehicle incorrectly listed as a repossession.
- √ A missing notation when you disputed a charge on a credit card bill.
- √ Accounts that incorrectly list you as a co-signer.
- √ Closed accounts incorrectly listed as open; it may look as though you have too much open credit.

- √ Accounts you closed that don't indicate closed by consumer—giving the false impression the creditor closed the account.
- √ An account delinquency that occurred more than seven years ago, or that does not include the date of the delinquency.
- √ Incorrect date of delinquency on an account that was charged off, or sent to collection, or the date of delinquency listed correctly on one account or trade line, but incorrectly on a second trade line after it was turned over to a collection agency—the transfer of a debt should not result in a new, later delinquency date.
- √ A creditor's trade line does not show that the account was turned over to a collection agency, so the collection agency account looks like another overdue account.
- √ Overdue child support that is more than seven years old.
- √ Other adverse information that is more than seven years old.

Inquiries

- √ Creditors cannot lawfully pull your credit report without your written permission, indicating a specific desire to obtain credit. They can obtain a soft inquiry which does not affect your score and you can check your credit score for free and it will never have an affect on your credit score
- √ Too many inquiries in a 12-month period can knock some points off your score. Never apply for anything unless you KNOW you will be approved.

How did that feel?

Many times, working with my clients on their reports, there are myriad feelings that surface: shock to see just how much of the information is incorrect, relieved to know there is a way to find the mistakes and have them corrected, and hope, that with the corrections being made—a brighter financial future is possible.

Doodle...

MIND-MAPPING IS a great way to get close and personal with your money and your credit. It is creative and fun and... opens you to emotions and realities you may have kept hidden for far too long! I know... I have talked about boundaries and coloring within the lines! Well, the only boundary you have on a mind-map is the edges of the page.

- √ Use this process to doodle out all the steps and tips you want to use on a daily basis to manage your money and credit more effectively.
- √ Use it to scribble out all the areas you feel you need to address to build stronger financial management skills.
- √ Use a mind-map to explore what you may need to build an emergency fund for.

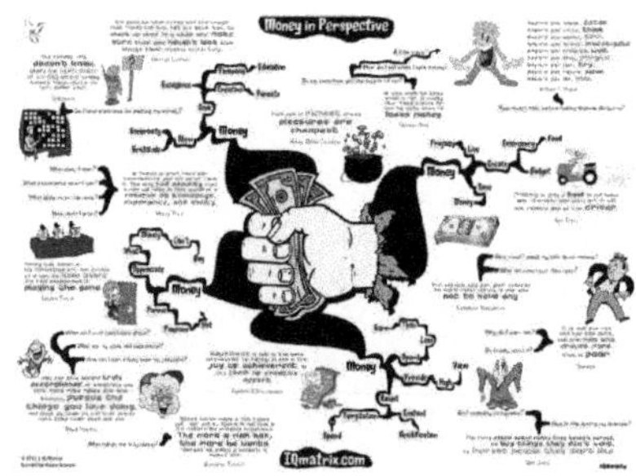

This image is shared to inspire you and help you understand the process; the task is to use the following page to doodle and allow your creativity to let it happen!

Image attribution: http://products.iqmatrix.com/money-perspective/

PHYSICAL EDUCATION

The great aim of education is not knowledge but action.

~ **Herbert Spencer** (1820-1903)
English author and philosopher

... not knowledge but action.

THE PHYSICAL EDUCATION classes you experienced in school were certainly colored differently than what you would expect of a credit report. But wait, what of the commonalities? Did not those classes teach you the importance and value of a physically active lifestyle? When you are actively engaged in anything, change happens; you cannot sit and wish and wonder and expect better personal health, social skills or motor skills. Likewise, you lose the credit game and your self-esteem if you do not actively participate in the financial matters that can negatively, or positively, impact your credit scores.

In keeping with the general intention of making sure *Color My Credit* is engaging and in some way, equally thought provoking and fun, the physical education class here is to rewrite your report; taking action in color! Use the guide that follows and take a deeper dive of connecting with the information in your credit report.

Action by Color

GREEN Great job! Keep it up. Ideally you have 3-4 green accounts.

RED Stop! Pay down all accounts to below 20%.

Credit card companies typically report once a month, and it is usually 7-10 days before your bill arrives in the mail. Call the creditor and inquire what day of the month they do report to the bureaus, or look on your credit report—you may be able to determine the "date last reported or updated." If so, put a reminder on your calendar to pay the card a few days prior to that date. An alternative, if you have a good payment history, is to call and request an increased limit. Either activity will lower the balance to limit ratio.

YELLOW You have slowed down—USE this card!

The card is possibly no longer being counted into the credit model algorithms. Don't forget to use it; putting a reminder on your calendar to rotate usage on your cards, to keep them in a "mix" that will increase your credit score.

PURPLE Not counted in credit model/algorithm.

Follow up on dispute; disputes will stay on the report until you ask for it to be removed.

Request method of debt verification from the credit bureaus after they have completed the dispute.

OR... remove it.

ORANGE These are the accounts you need to dispute, call and settle or set up a payment or request a pay and delete letter.

BLUE Not counted in credit model/algorithm.

Student loans or other accounts deferred.

No effect until they come out of deferment.

No action necessary.

Doodle...

I HOPE BY now you are feeling a little bit like I do, "There is an art to restoring you to good credit! My goal is to help you grasp the congruency between the lifestyle possible for you... and your credit scores. Every day of your life you are drawing a picture for someone else... to assess your credit worthiness! Every time you pay a bill, apply for credit, and open or close accounts... you color a different view.

Use the following page to doodle what you sense—right now in this moment—of the way FICO is interpreting your behavior. Make it colorful! Get out those crayons, and as Robert Fulghum so "colorfully" notes, "And we wouldn't go cheap, either—not little boxes of eight. Boxes of sixty-four, with the sharpener built right in. With silver and gold and copper, magenta and peach and lime, amber and umber and all the rest."

ENGLISH CLASS

One of the glories of English simplicity is the possibility of using the same word as noun and verb.

~**Edward Sapir** (1884-1939)
American scientist.

As you sit in English Class...

AH! ENGLISH CLASS... you either loved it or hated it. You either saw the overall picture or came away confused and overwhelmed. The stories either engaged you, or turned you off. The English class for *Color My Credit* is intended to be a little different and far easier. You see, you will find examples that remove any confusion or doubt; you will be able to master this class and make rapid changes in your credit score. For the most part, the examples will require only a little bit of "fill in the gaps" or "tell the tale" without a lot of colorful, flowery language. This is where you get to exercise the western adage, "Just the facts, ma'am—just the facts."

English, for the purposes of this class is about communication; not grammar. The following offers the materials and guidance you need, and a way to keep organized.

Data gathering and tasks assignment:

Name:

Current credit scores:

Transunion [ ] Experian [ ] Equifax [ ]

Goal: Get the mid-score above [ ]

Task(s)

Do not do anything with any trade line where the "date reported" is over 24-months; you will not want to consider touching it or it could drop your score.

Contact the collection companies and ask them to send you verification/documentation of the debt via fax or email. Do not make any payment if you feel the debt is not valid; you want to request proof of the debt sent to you.

Next step: The next step is to create the letters necessary for you to communicate with the credit bureaus. You will note the errors might not be listed on all three reports; send your request for change only to the bureau where you found it. Choose the letter from the samples included here in *Color My Credit* that most applies to your situation and double check the mailing address on the report you just pulled to make sure your communication goes to the right address.

Sample Dispute Letters

ON THE FOLLOWING pages you will find sample dispute letters for your convenience. Each serves a separate purpose, so choose wisely, depending on your needs. Working with my team and me in the future, you can have access to more guidance, direction, examples, and ultimately—positive results.

Sample Dispute Letter Re: Bankruptcy

Equifax
1550 Peachtree St
Atlanta, GA 30309

TransUnion
PO Box 2000
Chester, PA 19022

Experian
701 Experian Pkwy.
Allen, TX 85013

Date:

Sent Via Certified Mail—Return Receipt Requested

Dear Sir/Madam:

I was recently granted a bankruptcy discharge. As such all my accounts that were included in the bankruptcy should be reported on my credit report as **discharged in bankruptcy** and should be listed with a **zero balance.**

I have included a copy of my **Bankruptcy Discharge Order** from the court, as well as the **List of Creditors.** Please update my credit report. I am very concerned that this information is not updated correctly, it will have a damaging effect on my ability to rebuild my credit.

In addition, I am requesting a description of how the investigation was conducted, along with the name, address, and telephone number of anyone contacted for information.

My full name is...
My Social Security # is...
My date of birth is...
My home phone number is...
My address is...
City, State and Zip

I have enclosed a copy of **my identification** as proof of identity. Please send me an updated copy of my report and notification that items have been updated.

Sincerely
Your name...

Sample Dispute Letter to Credit Bureau

Date
Name
Street Address
City, State, and Zip

Name of Credit Bureau
Attn: Complaint Department
Street Address
City, State, and Zip

Re: Account Number

Dear Sir or Madam:

I am writing to dispute the following information in my file. The items I am disputing are circled on the enclosed copy of my report. *[Identify disputed items by source, such as creditor or agency, and note type of item, such as inquiries, credit card account, auto loan, legal judgment.]* These items are either inaccurate or incomplete, because *[describe the problem – fraud, unauthorized use, identity theft, etc.]*. I am requesting these items be deleted from my file *[or request another specific change]* to correct the information.

I am enclosing copies of *[describe supporting documents such as account statements, payment records, police reports, or ID Theft Affidavit]* supporting my claim. Please investigate this matter and correct the disputed items as soon as possible.

Sincerely,

Your name

Enclosures: *[List enclosed documents]*

Letter Re: Permission to communicate.

Your Name
Street Address
City, State, and Zip code

Date

Debt Collector Name
Street Address
City, State, and Zip code

Re: Account number for the debt—if you have it.

Dear [*Debt Collector Name]*:

I am responding to your contact about collecting a debt. You contacted me by [*phone, mail, email, etc.]* on [*date]* and identified the debt as [*any information they provided you about the debt.]*

You can contact me about this debt, but only in the way I state below. Do not contact me about this debt in any other manner, or at any other place or time. It is inconvenient for me to be contacted, except as I authorize below.

You can only contact me at:

[Mailing address *if you want physical mail.*]
[Phone number and convenient times, *if you want to be contacted by phone.]*

[IF correct, you can include the following] My employer prohibits me from receiving communications of this nature at my place of employment.

Thank you for your cooperation.

Sincerely,
[Your name]

Letter Re: Formal complaint of inaccurate information.

Your Name
Street Address
City, State, and Zip code

Date

Experian
PO Box 2002
Allen, TX 75013

TO WHOM IT MAY CONCERN:

This letter is a formal complaint that XXX COMPANY is reporting inaccurate credit information about me that is affecting my credit score.

I am very distressed you have included the information noted below in my credit profile due to its damaging effects on my good credit standing. As you are no doubt aware, credit-reporting laws ensure the bureaus report only accurate credit information. No doubt, the inclusion of this inaccurate information is a mistake on either your or the reporting creditor's part. Because of the mistakes on my credit report, I have been wrongfully denied credit recently for a mortgage, which was highly embarrassing, and has negative impacted my lifestyle.

With the proof I am attaching to this letter, I'm sure you'll agree it needs to be removed as soon as possible.

The following information needs to be verified and deleted from my credit report as soon as possible.

[*Account information from credit report; name, number, symbols, etc.*]

Please delete the above information as quickly as possible.

Sincerely,
Name

GETTING THE HOMEWORK DONE

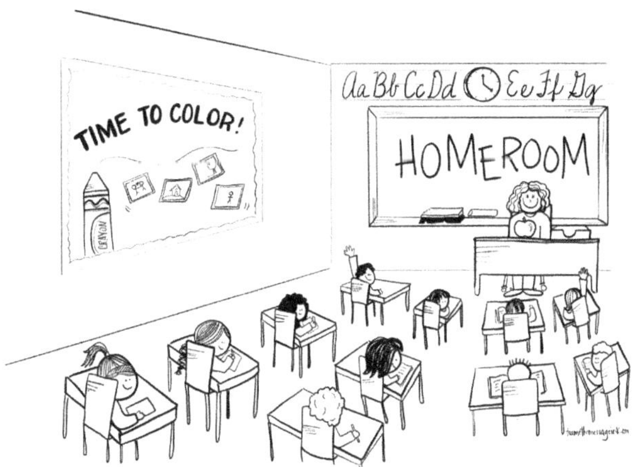

One of life's most painful moments comes when we must admit that we didn't do our homework, that we are not prepared.

~ **Merlin Olsen** (1940-2010)
American Athlete.

Financial Checklist

Nope! You don't get away without doin' the work! The only way to move forward through something that blocks you from a better place in life is to go over, under, around or through it! So, that is exactly what I am going to challenge you to do by completing the homework listed below.

Don't panic! You can work your way through it and reach out and ask for help if you reach a limitation you cannot bust through. You will just need to keep your eye on the prize—a much-improved FICO score that opens the doors for the lifestyle you desire and will have earned.

You will also notice that not all these action steps will apply to your current circumstances; however, I encourage you to review each of them, and know that in future, if your circumstances change, you will know exactly what you need to do to prepare yourself for an exciting change in your life.

New Grad, entering the workforce...

- √ Make a budget
- √ Track your expenses
- √ Pay down your debt
- √ Start saving for retirement
- √ Designate beneficiaries on your financial accounts
- √ Start your estate planning
- √ Get disability insurance

Career advancement…

- √ When you switch jobs—negotiate salaries.
- √ Take your retirement funds with you.
- √ Start working with a fee-based financial planner with an eye on retirement.

Getting married…

- √ Create—or update—your will, and update all beneficiaries, powers of attorney, health-care proxies, etc.
- √ Look into getting life insurance, and re-evaluate other insurance policies.

Buying a home…

- √ Buy a home that does not put undue stress on your assets.
- √ If you are married, and have not purchased life insurance, look into it now... and update your disability insurance.

Having children…

- √ Review your estate plan.
- √ Start saving for college education(s).
- √ Relay financial lessons to your children.
- √ Established in your career…
- √ Max out your retirement contributions.
- √ Be proactive in your tax planning.
- √ If you find yourself taking care of your parents, consider their needs in the context of your financial priorities.

- √ Begin planning your retirement income.
- √ If need be, catch up on retirement contributions.

Retirement...

- √ Know your budget—as adjusted for retirement.
- √ Review your investments, and how they will play into your retirement plans.
- √ Consider down-sizing.
- √ Look at funding potential long-term care costs.

Survivor...

- √ Don't make any immediate changes following the loss of your loved one.
- √ Review your estate plan to best manage changes created by the loss of your loved one.
- √ Downsize, and consider moving into a full retirement community.
- √

Doodle...

HOW WOULD YOU like to have lots of fun doodling away your credit card debt—in far less time than you would ever imagine? It is time to stop dragging all that debt around with you and need a better approach than calling in a bevy of unicorns saddled with bags of cash... the fun comes in the nature of an inexpensive set of sharpie colored pens and a piece of inexpensive stretched canvas, or any doodle image such as this, which somehow inspires you. Let the image represent your goal—debt reduction. When you meet a particular smaller goal, color in one of the shapes on your art project.

Grab your sharpie, go online and download a free doodle or just create your own by adding lines and shapes on stretched canvas, and start documenting your debt reduction! You can choose to color in a portion of your image for every $25, $50, or $100 goal you achieve. Not only does this technique help you "own" your debt, but creates a visual of the success you are achieving with each of those small payments. You are also welcome to hurry over to the resources page on my website where you will find links to sites offering free, downloadable doodles, like this… or have fun drawing your own!

LOVIN' THE LIBRARY

The library is the temple of learning, and learning has liberated more people than all the wars in history.

~ **Carl T. Rowan** (1925-2000)
American author and journalist.

The Temple of Learning

I'M NOT SURE what your earliest memories are about libraries, but go with me here on a little visionary journey! Think of a warm summer afternoon, setting aside busy family noises and activities... escaping as you walk to the local library. Inside, you relax in the quiet—with no fear of interruption—wrapped in a rather contagious sense of safety within its walls. Look around you and watch the small beings at scaled-down child desks—almost cartoonish in size—where picture books are carefully arranged atop faded, scuffed wooden tables.

Now move forward to junior high and high school and remember how you shifted from the safety you felt in elementary school, to a fascination with myriad "library tools," which helped you efficiently complete demanding school papers. Now, fast forward to college... remember how it offered an odd flavor of a tiny, pocket-sized, dark library that wrapped you not in the safety of childhood, but a chilling despair in the certainty you might never manage writing high-level papers.

Our credit lives are much like that library... we equally find comfort, fascination and despair! Today, you can the childhood feelings again, knowing that when I published

Color My Credit I have given back... I have placed a valuable book **on the shelf** rather than relive my lifetime experience of removing them.

I hope this visionary library experience has also been pleasant, and that as you hold *Color My Credit* in your hands you will find the weight of the books calming; your pleasure piqued by understanding of how—just as in school—the pages offer to transform you. Read on and enjoy learning the congruency of color and credit.

Storytime...

Do Over

I MET JULIE four years ago at a homeless shelter when I was working for a church ministry. We had an immediate deep connection and it was difficult to not embrace her two children; they just had a special light about them. She had just left an abusive marriage and was trying to find her way back and at the end of the class we had a very touching conversation with one of us, I am not sure which, saying, "Wow, I think we have truly developed a special heart connection. It would be great to stay in touch.

I don't think we did a great job of staying as closely in touch as we had anticipated, but our years later, I was hosting a *Color My Credit* workshop in my office and not one person attended. My heart was heavy and filled with a great sadness as I started cleaning up the room, but that all disappeared when I recognized Julie entering the room, and even more so when she said, "Oh, am I glad... really grateful no one else showed for your class!" I know that sounds bad, but I am having some real social anxiety, not to mention how overwhelmed I am to think about looking at my credit. You see, day before yesterday I went online and printed off my credit report like you advised in the flyer for the class!

I was excited she had seen the flyer, and printed her report, and showed up for the class, but my heart almost broke at hearing her next sentence.

"I have to tell you, Alisa, I started crying when the printer got to page 120. I guess all that represented to me was having to come face-to-face with all the failures in my life—you know, all those things I really didn't have the courage to face."

You can well imagine my delight when Julie handed the lengthy report to me and boldly stated, "Ok, talk me through this."

I sat down at the conference table where I had anticipated there would have been 10-12 eager students, realizing I was happy to have this one. But as I browsed through her pages, I became puzzled. Page, after page I turned and finally turned to Julie and asked, "Did you look at this?"

Her response came from a place of deep brokenness, "I tried to, but I just know it's all bad. I just can't comprehend what it all means."

I stood up and went to my computer and within just a few minutes I had her mortgage credit report—with scores—and exclaimed, "Just as I suspected! You have a 729 middle FICO score!

Julie's mouth dropped as tears rolled down her face. She said, "I just assumed my past would never let me move forward."

After I pointed out to Julie that her credit score was based on the last 24 months of her life, not her entire life history and because she had taken my advice and opened the two secured credit cards using less than 20% of the limit and getting a car loan reporting with no late payments, the GOOD eventually outweighed the bad. And the same was true for Julie's life that day moving forward.

We ALL have the ability for a DO OVER. You just have to show up!

Not only did Julie have a 729, she had been at the same job for two years and was able to qualify for a $175k house. Because her credit score was above 640, she was also able to get approved for a grant giving her $20k to cover her down payment and closing costs. She was finally going to be able to get a home she and those precious children would own and provide more stability for them.

As she left my office, I asked, "So, Julie, are you planning on staying with Home Depot?"

She was quiet for a few moments, but finally responded, saying, "Yes, but Alisa, I am thinking maybe one day I can help others and show them that I did it and they can too!"

I smiled deep inside, knowing she would and left the office feeling I had just had the most successful turnout for a workshop—ever. The story didn't end there... Julie closed on a gorgeous home for $180k 60 days later, with no money required for the down payment, and for the first time, her children had a home to call their own... in a nice neighborhood.

Learning Through Color...

WE ARE ALL born with a reticular activator, which by way of easy explanation is the part of our brains that stays on alert. It has the important job of helping you notice certain things and ignore others. Just think about how distracted you would be if you actually noticed everything—it would be impossible to function!

How do you know when your reticular activator is at work? My friend shared a story of her grandson who was just positive there were no purple cars manufactured. Wanting to teach him about how this special part of the brain works, she challenged him to count on it to see just how many purple cars he would *notice* when he thought there were none. Imagine his surprise when at the end of the week he had *noticed* 37 purple cars! Another example is how motivational speakers and business consultants stress the importance of having a goal; the intent is to implant the thought that will trigger your reticular activator to be highly receptive to your personal objectives (goals).

When I was first inspired to write *Color My Credit,* I started noticing things I had never noticed before. It seemed like the world was suddenly conspiring to help me out. I started meeting just the right people. I ran into the perfect designer for my cover and was introduced to a literary strategist to keep me on the right path, and connected at a deeper level with people from my previous career in the comedy field to participate in launching my project!

Is it amazing coincidences, reticular activator, or divine intervention? I am open to all three! I just know all these things happened, and continue occurring because I have a clear goal of what I want and all things cooperate to help me achieve it.

For the most part, we tend to run on auto-pilot. We manage to think the way we have always thought, notice the things we've always noticed, and overlook things we've always overlooked. However...

> when you have a new awareness of a particular thing—you start noticing things you would normally overlook—and that begins to make all the difference!

Why do I bring this particular topic to your mind? Because it is exactly what happened to transform my life in a way that allows me to help you make positive changes in your own! Color My Credit™ was one of those things that got stuck in my reticular activator. It opened my own awareness to the very problem it now serves to solve; it revealed to me there was a different way to look at improving lives by being a change agent, advocating for those in credit despair; and it created a new belief that color is a powerful—and empowering—tool for learning. Which leads me into the information I am about to share with you. You see, I wasn't deliberately "looking" for information on using color as a learning tool... it showed up to support my innate belief that color was what I was to use for my passion to change the world, to change lives... one credit score at a time.

I need to give credit for the awareness of learning through color to Cercone Learning. To avoid plagiarism, I will summarize what I have learned, but because there is merit in sharing some of the information in direct quotes, they are placed in italics.

The first thing I learned through Cercone was an understanding of what color is and how it actually works in our brains. Essentially, as we learned as children, color is part of what we know as the electromagnetic spectrum. As vital energy, each and every color has a magnetic frequency and specific wavelength. As a biochemical response... color affects the neuropathways in our brains.

What I found interesting, and necessary to the Color My Credit Method, is that most people lack the essential neuropathway connections necessary to learning for a number of reasons:

√ Lack of sufficient time in creeping and crawling, which develops the brain. Creeping and crawling connect neuropathways.

√ Food allergies and deficiencies in minerals and vitamins.

√ Other emotional and mental stresses.

In addition to what I found at Cercone Learning, other areas of research have been completed— relative to just how the brain develops from birth forward. In my expansive and fascinating reading, it became evident virtually every movement and its effect on a child has been studied! Some of the studies address how movement helps the brain develop—much in the manner a child's physical body grows and develops over many years.

One of the major discoveries was that if a child's *natural movements* are unnaturally delayed or activated too soon, the brain then lacks the proper development and connectivity necessary for **both** general learning and coordination in sports. One of my friends validated this concept by sharing how her son walked far earlier than normal... totally skipping the crawling process. In first grade the child's teacher noticed his lack of coordination, and aware of the implication on his learning capacity, had his parents get down on their hands and knees and engage him in crawling activities... to bring his brain development up to speed! It may interest you to know this same child became an astro-physicist!

Consider children who are slow in school or fail one particular subject; it is clearly evident, from what I learned from Cercone and other resources, a particular neuropathway was not developed or connected. You can draw the analogy of trying to use the electricity in your home when the wires are down… no matter how many times you flip that switch, there is simply no light.

This is where my learning became exciting! I discovered if for example, a child has reading problems, giving them more reading exercise time in most cases will not solve the problem. Fortunately, if the **correct color** is found for an individual's problem "subject" it becomes much easier and the student experiences success and increased confidence. This awareness immediately reminded me of Albert Einstein's all too familiar quote,

We need to use a different type of thinking than the thinking that created the problem.

Think back to when you were in school… if you recall your classmates you probably can place them in one of two categories: some who struggled and others who just found learning unbelievably easy. If you consider those who did excel in their class subjects, you probably will remember they were extremely coordinated in other activities, and in thinking back—you probably thought, *Dang! Everything comes easy to them!*

One of the case studies I read in the Cercone materials addressed an outstanding student whose abilities piqued the interest of the instructor. Upon having conversations with the parents, the teacher discovered the child crawled forever… the parents feared the child would never walk.

The conclusion drawn by the teacher was that because of the natural brain development, color was not as critical a learning tool for this child as for many of the other students. However, when color was used, this student learned faster, remembered more easily, and she was more effortlessly motivated when the use of color made learning more fun.

According to Cercone, color is a key element to open and connect the 12 human intelligence factors.

> Color *helps concepts become more logical.*
>
> Color *opens the mathematical process, makes reasoning and memory easier.*
>
> Color *opens creativity.*
>
> *Any scientific subject becomes much easier through the use of color.*
>
> Color *can help meet the challenges facing over 200 million Americans and millions in other countries.*
>
> *When knowledge on the planet is doubled every few years, when continuing education is now a must, not a luxury, color is a most critical and important tool to achieve personal success, corporate success and a global success in which we reach out to help each other.*
>
> Color *is a frequency that can connect and create a neuropathway that allows that subject or movement to become so much easier and allows learning to be faster and memory to go deeper.*

I also loved the likeness in Cercone's work to a student named Casey, who when playing piano with the projection of colored light noted, “It feels like my hands are finally connected to my brain.”

The next stage to increase my awareness about all these almost magical color possibilities was finding just how color works. I mean, once you know that something can be so powerful, isn’t the next natural step finding out how to make it work for you? I needed to learn why, when concert tickets are printed in one color for the Friday matinee and another color for Saturday’s main performance, people become conditioned to look at the color of their ticket to make sure they attend the right event rather than sorting out the exact day. What I learned... the brain sees and remembers color first!

Cercone Learning promotes the belief color is a powerful stimulus for the brain, which opens up other areas of the brain, allowing for easier learning through the process of connecting between the 12 intelligences as previously noted. I am cognizant of how this might play into the *Color My Credit Method*... what if I had a student who truly felt they could read the material, yet simply not comprehend the information?

What if I could find the right color, which when laid over the reading material—could change one of my student’s outcomes?

The following examples from the Cercone studies tell a proving tale...

Red for Physics: One of the students portrayed had good grades in virtually every class… except physics, which just didn't happen for him. When tested for color, it was discovered that a vibrant red changed the results for this high school senior. Unfortunately, his teenaged ego set in and the student refused to use the filter. He knew the possibilities, but only when he got frustrated enough with bad grades holding the key to his future, did he come back to the center asking help to understand just how the process worked. He decided to set aside his perceived embarrassment, used the red filter, and subsequently completed not only high school but earned a Master's Degree.

Another case study discussed an adult who was concerned she could not remember material for longer than five minutes. She agreed to be color tested, used the color that worked for her and upon returning a week later, was ecstatic to share she had read the morning paper and for the first time in her life was able to remember what she had read.

I loved the poignancy of this story:

"I want to write, but the paper grabs my pencil."

Jonathan had a very curious mind and wanted to explore many things. He came to me one day because he loved to write but when he wrote, the "paper grabbed the pencil."

His mother and I looked at him quizzically, but that was the best explanation he could give. I first tested him with a colored filter and a white paper and black pen. When we got to a shade of blue filter, he exclaimed: "The paper does not grab the pencil with this color."

I proceeded to find a colored paper that was the same shade as the blue filter and he chose a certain shade of blue pen to write with. Now he could write to his heart's content with ease!

"The ideas just keep coming!"

Another child had serious problems skipping words in her reading and spent laborious time re-reading just so she could understand. This played part I am sure, to her lack of confidence in expressing herself in writing. Once tested for these two issues, reading through filtered colors of dusty blue and lavender resolved the word skipping and by writing on colored paper, with a colored pen, her thoughts flowed to the paper like water.

As I continued reading the stories, one after another, I didn't really want to stop. They inspired me!

What can I do for the world if I use the power of color for the credit students who come through my classes?

The techniques presented by Cercone ran the gamut... from writing on colored paper to testing responses to various shades of colored pencils or crayons. One rather unique tip was to create to-do lists in color and instead of crossing them off when completed, get creative and color them to express your pleasure!

The color testing gels, which are not available to the general public are available at Cercone's website: www.cerconelearning.com

Other tips include the use of multiple-colored highlighters, taking notes in color, and even organizing various paragraphs or topics by color. These tips inspire me; they remind me of the amazing work of the author, SARK, who crafts every page of her books in wild, beautiful colors! When I think about what I remember from SARK's books, I am intrigued to see how much of it is in green—according to what I learned from Cercone, *the brain remembers the color first and the color then activates the memory.*

What I saw as a tagline for Cercone was,

Enjoy coloring your life!

I contend we will move forward, coloring our credit! I truly applaud you for going the distance here with me. I trust it enhanced your awareness of color and understand my passion to use it in every layer of the *Color My Credit Method.*

As we move through the balance of our time in the library, enjoy and engage in the materials placed on the top of your scaled-down child desk—almost cartoonish in size—where pages of *Color My Credit* are carefully opened—atop a faded, scuffed wooden table!

Sample Credit Reports

THE FOLLOWING IMAGE is provided, just to increase your awareness of the type of information provided on your credit report. Since there are so many versions available, only a small snipped is provided. You will learn far more when you actually download your free annual report and begin to discover many things you probably never even knew existed.

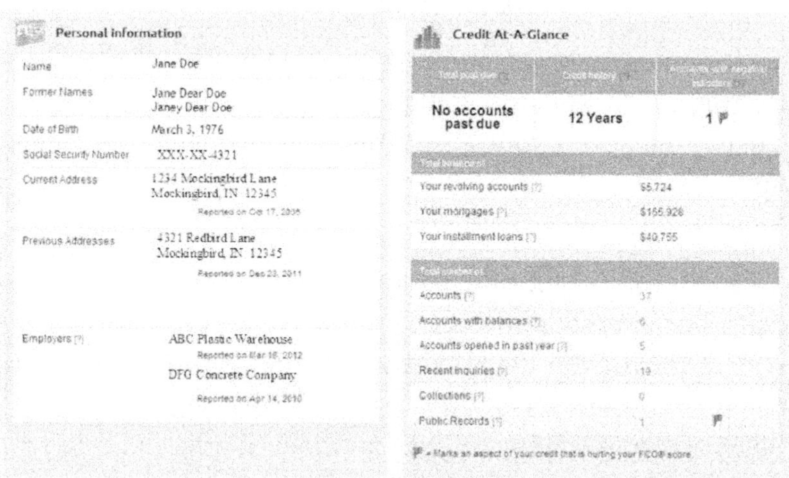

Personal information

Name	Jane Doe
Former Names	Jane Dear Doe Janey Dear Doe
Date of Birth	March 3, 1976
Social Security Number	XXX-XX-4321
Current Address	1234 Mockingbird Lane Mockingbird, IN 12345 Reported on Oct 17, [illegible]
Previous Addresses	4321 Redbird Lane Mockingbird, IN 12345 Reported on Dec 23, 2011
Employers [?]	ABC Plastic Warehouse Reported on Mar 16, 2012 DFG Concrete Company Reported on Apr 14, 2010

Credit At-A-Glance

[illegible]	[illegible]	[illegible]
No accounts past due	12 Years	1

[illegible]		
Your revolving accounts [?]	$5,724	
Your mortgages [?]	$165,926	
Your installment loans [?]	$40,755	

[illegible]		
Accounts [?]	37	
Accounts with balances [?]	6	
Accounts opened in past year [?]	5	
Recent inquiries [?]	19	
Collections [?]	0	
Public Records [?]	1	

= Marks an aspect of your credit that is hurting your FICO® score

Three-Bureau Information

THERE WILL BE times when you will need to contact one or all of the bureaus to request necessary modifications to your report. The following addresses were current at the time of this writing; it is a good idea to double-check the address by going to the website if you have an old version of this book.

CREDIT REPORTING AGENCIES

Equifax Credit Information Services
P.O. Box 740241
Atlanta, GA 30374-0241
800-685-1111
www.equifax.com

Experian (Formerly TRW)
P.O. Box 2104
Allen, TX 75013-2104
888- EXPERIAN (397-3742)
http://www.experian.com

Trans Union Corporation
Consumer Relations Division
P.O. Box 390
Springfield, PA 19064-0390
800-888-4213
www.transunion.co

Consumer Credit Laws

BEING WELL INFORMED is your best guard and tool against having a low FICO score. The following consumer credit laws are important—need to know—vital pieces of information, which you will want to review and refer to from time to time as you have questions about why certain actions toward creditors are allowed by law. Sometimes the protection is actually intended for you!

Risk-Based Pricing Rule (2011), issued in accordance with an amendment to the Fair Credit Reporting Act, is intended to: increase the level of transparency in the lending process, raise the awareness that your credit history is being used to set credit terms offered by lenders, and further improve the accuracy of information maintained by credit reporting agencies. Today consumers who receive Risk-based Pricing notices from lenders will find the credit score that was used in making the credit decision included in their notice.

Credit CARD Act (2009) provides important consumer credit protections.

Fair and Accurate Credit Transactions Act (2003), an amendment to the Fair Credit Reporting Act, allows consumers to request and obtain a free credit report once every twelve months from each of the three nationwide consumer credit reporting companies.

Credit Repair Organizations Act (1996) prohibits a variety of false and misleading statements, as well as fraud by credit repair organizations.

Fair Credit and Charge Card Disclosure Act (1988) requires a lender offering you a credit card to tell you about certain terms on the card, including the annual percentage rate (APR), the amount of any annual fee and whether you have an interest-free period to pay your bill before any interest charges are added. See also Truth in Lending Act.

Fair Debt Collection Practices Act (1977) details the rules a debt collector must follow when trying to collect a debt. It prohibits collectors from engaging in abusive collection practices such as calling outside of the hours of 8:00 a.m. to 9:00 p.m. local time, or communicating with you at work after they have been advised that this is unacceptable or prohibited by the employer.

Equal Credit Opportunity Act (1974) prohibits discrimination in credit transactions on the basis of certain personal characteristics including race, color, religion, national origin, sex, marital status, age, being a recipient of public assistance or exercising your rights under the Consumer Credit Protection Act.

Fair Credit Billing Act (1974) requires that a credit card company promptly credits your payments and corrects mistakes on your bill without damage to your credit score. It also lets you dispute credit card billing errors and withhold payment for damaged goods. See also Truth in Lending Act below.

Fair Credit Reporting Act (1970) protects you against inaccurate or misleading information in credit files maintained by credit reporting agencies. It requires that you must be told what's in your credit file and have the ability to correct any errors. The **Risk-Based Pricing Rule** implements section 615 (h) of the Fair Credit Reporting Act.

Consumer Credit Protection Act (1969) is an umbrella consumer protection law that includes the Equal Credit Opportunity Act, the Fair Credit Billing Act, the Fair Credit Reporting Act, Credit Repair Organizations Act, and the Truth in Lending Act.

Truth in Lending Act (1968) requires that lenders use uniform methods for computing the cost of credit and for disclosing credit terms so that you can tell how much it will cost to borrow money. It also limits your liability to $50 if your credit card is lost, stolen, or used without your authorization, and it prohibits the unsolicited issuance of credit cards. The Fair Credit Billing Act and the Fair Credit and Charge Card Disclosures Act were later additions to the Truth in Lending Act, as are many provisions of the Credit CARD Act.

And the stories continue...

DO YOU REMEMBER when you were in kindergarten and the lower grades how the teacher would trek you all—quietly and in single file—down to the library where you would sit—quietly—in a circle while she, or the librarian read you such captivating stories? Well, no single-file or sitting on the floor today, but I do have a story to share with you, titled *The Lucky Guy!*

Joe and Julie are two graduates from Arizona State University- Both are 21 and each has built the same credit profile... they have the same credit card limit and they both max out their credit cards each month but don't worry because they pay them off in full every month.

Joe found out the date his credit card reports to the credit bureaus and marked his calendar to pay the balance the day *before* they report (which is about 7-10 days usually before the bill arrives in the mail, although they are all different). Julie didn't know that so she pays, like everyone else, when the bill comes in the mail. The creditor reports that Joe uses under 20% of his credit utilization every month and Julie is at 100%. Joe's mid credit score for a mortgage 720, Julie's 620.

Joe and Julie apply for the same job; same qualifications... but Joe gets it because his *credit report looks less risky.* Joe becomes Julie's boss, even though they have the same education. Joe makes 60k. Julie makes 40k.

They both decide to apply for a mortgage. Joe is able to obtain a 200k house on a 15 year fixed in a nice neighborhood. Julie also buys a 200k home in the same neighborhood on a 30 year fixed mortgage. However, because of Joe's great credit score his interest rate, home insurance and mortgage insurance are lower and the difference in payment is $142 less a month than Julie's 30-year loan.

Joe takes out a car loan at 3% interest due to his score. Julie gets 9% for her interest rate. Same exact car—same exact price. Julie's car insurance is $100 more a month than Joe. Her car payment is $100 more than Joe's monthly payment due to the rate.

At the end of 15 years, Joe owns his home free and clear. Julie still owes 135k and she *still* has car loans because she can never get ahead to save any money.

...she has never felt *confident* asking for a raise due to how unworthy she feels from not getting the job she wanted in the first place.

...she has had to *rely on credit cards* to make ends meet due to her income and is always maxed out on her cards which continues to drive her scores down.

Buried in debt, Julie cashes out her 401k to get back on top, takes out huge penalties and manages to take what she has left to build towards retirement, which isn't much.

And because Joe's confidence built year over year after getting that first job, he goes on to be a National Public Speaker and speaks at life changing conferences where Julie just arrived this morning.

And it started with one date.

Doodle...

IF YOU WERE to make good credit a game, what would it look like to you? Use the space below to doodle in what that image represents to you. Something like Monopoly? Go PIG? What could you engage in to make the process more fun; make it a game?

Section II

The Indomitable Credit Report

I know a baseball star who wouldn't report the theft of his wife's credit cards because the thief spends less than she does.

~ **Joe Garagiola** (1926-2016)
Professional baseball player and sports announcer.

But first—take time for a SONG...

It's All About My Score

(sung to the tune of All About That Bass by Meghan Trainor)

Because you know I'm
All about my score
About my score
My Credit...

It's all about my score
About my score
My Credit...

Well, it's pretty clear I have an 802
Because I charge it; pay it
That's what you're supposed to do
I got that score all the banks chase
I pay all the right bills to all the right places.
You see those credit sites
That say, "Dispute, non-stop!"
You know that stuff don't work.
Come on, now, make it stop!
If you got knowledge, knowledge...
You can raise it up
Everyone can raise their score from the bottom to the top.

Yeah, my momma she told me, "Don't worry about your score,"
But you'll be more successful if you don't choose to ignore.
Yeah, I won't be no airhead, hanging out at the mall.

Color My Credit | Alisa Glutz

No money, money…
No, I'll buy me a house and pay all my credit cards off…
Just don't close them!

Because you know it's all about my score
About my score
My Credit…

It's all about my score
About my score
My Credit… (Repeat 2x)

I'm bringing POWER back….
Tell all those collectors that…
"You know I'd like to chat"…..
"But you broke three rules I know so that collection has to go."

Chapter 1
The Importance of Credit Education

NOW, ALTHOUGH MY silly little song was intentionally designed to put a little fun into a very serious topic, by no means do I want you to undervalue the importance of your credit score or the importance of credit education. In 2015 I was honored to have been chosen to speak about my passion for learning to manage money matters and leave a financial legacy, but I have to admit I got a little carried away with my pitch. Have you ever done something like that… pitching a client or other professional why they should work with you and—oops—accidently say something you all of a sudden realize, *Oh! Now I am going to have to back this up later!*

As I explained my desire to speak about credit education, I could feel my conversation fading. I also realized talking about credit and credit scores is most often perceived as b-o-r-i-n-g so out of nowhere, I proclaimed, "Oh, and I write mortgage business parody songs!" I think subconsciously I figured the statement would slip away and be forgotten before I was called upon to speak, but oh, no! Month after month, in preparation for the speech, it was somehow advertised that there was going to be a little surprise during my presentation.

Before we get to that, however, I want to spend a few minutes sharing with you just why you should make credit education one of your biggest goals. Much like Dorothy in the Wizard of Oz, 2008 took Americans through a financial tornado causing millions to experience financial woes, with many losing their homes.

... the house has stopped spinning now, but just like Dorothy emerged from her own storm, the financial world we face has changed; it looks much different.

I imagine many of you were there in 2008, watching people around you losing their homes, with the devastating realization there was little to be done to resolve a growing problem. Now, as the dust begins to settle, American communities are looking for someone to guide them home again. As an industry leader, whether you serve in the area of real estate or financial services, or are trying to find your own way...

Color My Credit is the yellow brick road to follow and with brains (education), heart (encouragement) and courage we will make our way back to Emerald City!

In the second quarter of 2010 the charge-off rate on credit card debt went literally through the roof. Charge-offs typically occur about 180 days from the date of first non-payment. What many people don't realize is derogatory debt stays on your credit for seven years from the date of first delinquency. This is predicated on the fact that many people would be eligible to use credit again over the next five years, but the greater question is whether they will be credit ready.

The key is to know which items are being reflected on a credit report and whether what is reported is accurate.

What you learn in *Color My Credit* is how to be prepared, get credit ready, and become credit worthy once again.

INSIDER TIP: THERE ARE AN UNBELIEVABLE AMOUNT OF ERRORS BEING UNCOVERED IN CONSUMER CREDIT REPORTS! IT TAKES A DEEP DIVE TO SEPARATE WHAT IS FOUND IN A TRI-MERGED CREDIT REPORT, JUST TO SEE AND COMPARE WHAT EACH BUREAU IS REALLY REPORTING.

A quick look back, and we see the 18 year-olds caught in the fallout of 2008 are now in their late twenties. They are of the age to purchase a home and start a family, but guess what? While the Credit Card Act of 2009 had HUGE benefits to consumers, anyone under the age of 21 stopped being eligible to secure credit without income documentation or having mom and dad co-sign for them. What were mom and dad doing in 2009? Losing their homes and retirement savings during the housing crisis. There was no co-signing for junior; in fact mom and dad had to encourage the use of student loans because they needed every resource just to manage their own financial affairs. The result?

A large number of consumers with thin credit files, and lots of deferred and non-deferred student loans, resulting in a highly-blemished credit file.

Let's take a short segue here and look more carefully at a well known, but not so well understood document: the credit report.

This action is critical because much of the time, the discrepancies are significant. In fact, over the past few years, the conversations I have had with my clients is not so much about what they owe, or how much they should pay, but whether the transactions are reported accurately. You can feel better about the face of your credit, knowing **The Fair Credit Reporting Act** protects you from information being inaccurately reported. I am so passionate about the work I do because it raises the question I would love you to ask if you serve consumers, "How does helping others with their credit—essentially for free—help generate more business for me?" Stop and think about the memorable quote by the late, highly revered, Zig Ziglar, "You can have everything you want in life, if you will just help enough other people get what they want."

Although much of this short portion of information is directed to service professionals, it is included in Color My Credit because of its ultimate benefit to you as a consumer who is committed to improving your financial status.

I want to start a movement... shifting the perspective and use of credit within our nation—starting in my industry and the communities whom I serve.

This movement must begin with educating our communities, friends and family about the use of credit, and credit cards in particular. Let me start by being firm in my belief credit cards are not the enemy! Nor should they be considered as ready cash. When used properly, credit cards are a great tool for moving your credit score. Don't foolishly cut them up because you haven't been able to manage them.

Discover your boundaries, color inside the lines, and learn how to make them work to create the picture of life you want.

Credit Tip: *If the limit on your card is $1,000—drop the last zero—and use that figure ($100) for your TRUE monthly spending limit. If you use the card for business; pay it off in full each month or leave a balance below the TRUE limit.*

INSIDER SECRET: KNOW WHEN IT IS BEST TO PAY YOUR CREDIT CARD BALANCE EACH MONTH—IT IS NOT YOUR DUE DATE

Why? Credit cards typically report 7-10 days **before** your bill arrives in the mail each month. When do you

typically make that payment? Either when you get the bill or just before the due date.

The date that matters to you is when the company reports the card to each bureau.

How do you discover when your card is being reported? Simple! Call the company and ask, or go to: www.annualcreditreport.com and look for the date last updated on Transunion and Equifax reports. Experian only provides the month and year.

What steps do you take? Once you identify the date last updated or reported, put an auto-reminder in your calendar or phone three or more days prior to that updated date and pay the card in full if possible instead of waiting for your bill to arrive. This simple move changes the date paid to prior to the reporting and can, as it has done for myriad of my personal clients, help move credit scores over 100 points in as little as 30-60 days.

Let me share another little story with you that will show you just how important this one little *insider tip* can be to best manage your financial legacy.

I call it my ***Millionaire's Mistake***!

About a year ago, I had four clients call me over a weekend to purchase homes. Now, they were all wealthy people who wanted to purchase million dollar homes, but none wanted to hear anything about how my credit knowledge would benefit them—until I pulled their credit reports. Each of them was of the understanding they had scores in the high 700s. Imagine their surprise—perhaps dismay—when the scores were in the low 600's stemming from a late pay within the past 30 days. None felt they had been late before so they contacted the creditor and requested a *goodwill removal* of the late pay, and each was successful. With the recent 30-day late removed, all four of the parties' mid-scores increased by roughly 100 points.

Why was this so important? Large banks assess your credit-worthiness and you are either denied credit, or given a higher interest rate based on the derogatory reporting.

These millionaires had been turned down for a pretty basic credit request!

You can imagine how good I felt about following Zig Ziglar's premise of helping others when I was able to close over three million dollars in home sales by helping four people in one weekend, and all I had to do was boldly declare my credit education for their overall benefit. The real score for me however, was also educating the luxury real estate agents who initially had felt my knowledge was not necessary for their wealthy clients. Not only am I known for my knowledge and the changes it makes, but professional real estate agents count on me to connect with them on a personal level. At my own professional level, more and more of my time is spent serving referrals than marketing for new clients... my passion for transforming financial legacies now precedes me.

FICO mortgage scores have long been the bane of consumers and the service professionals who work to secure financing for them.

In 1995, major players, Fannie Mae and Freddie Mac decided to use FICO scores to approve, decline, or adjust rates for mortgage loans—at which time the game plan began to be helping clients shift their score over the hump so to speak. Fast forward, and today we find the game plan not always so successful if the last 24 months reporting have any derogatory credit issues reflected. Let me tell you another short story so this has more meaning...

The following story shows how I was able to help a couple buy a home by reviewing a recent credit report, and improving their *date of last activity.*

The Dilemma of Dick and Delores

The couple wanted to buy a home in the next few months, but both their FICO scores were short of what I needed to gain the approval and/or best product and rate. The debt ratio was fine, but they had no extra cash to draw from—we had a dilemma!

Back to the credit report I went to see what we might be able to take advantage of and I found a credit card for Victoria's Secret that had not been used in over two years. I got excited and quickly called, asking, "Do you still have the Victoria Secret credit card that you could use?"

Her response got me even more excited, "Oh, my gosh! I had forgotten all about it. Let me check my wallet. Yes! I do have it here, why?"

I knew she was feeding off my growing excitement, when I delivered my request, "Ok. I need you to take some time this weekend and slip over to the store and make a small purchase. And, while you are there request to have your husband added as an authorized user."

The task was done, and the credit card was brought into the *current mix*, bringing her score up by 30 points; her husband's score increased by 40 points once he was added as the authorized user and it showed on his credit report 30 days later. The couple was able to close on the home of their dreams and their marriage is better than ever... all because we were able to move the *date of last activity*—and perhaps a little help by additional purchases at Victoria Secret!

I work on a daily basis with other real estate and financial services professionals who rely on the knowledge I share with them to respond to home ownership credit issues like I just shared with you here. It fascinates me how easily these three simple steps can unlock the key to the happy marriage between credit and home ownership.

1. Understand how to use credit cards as *tools* to improve credit scores.
2. Discover the importance of what you might consider a simple 30-day late.

3. Focus on the last 24 months of credit report information to assess *date opened, date reported, and date of last activity.*

Chapter 2
Reading the Credit Report

THERE ARE MYRIAD elements on a credit report to read and try to figure out, and since each consumer has a vastly different picture that has colored their world, this chapter is designed to cover some of the more important areas. You will read about how to manage disputes, correct errors, and a short little "skinny" on how creditors generally report.

Account Status—Disputes

ALL CREDIT BUREAUS allow you to dispute mistakes via mail and over the telephone; however, experience shows me it is best to dispute credit report errors online. Each of the three major bureaus we have discussed offer online dispute resolutions services, which are faster and far more streamlined than using snail mail or speaking to someone via phone. Just make sure to upload to their website written documentation you have to support your dispute, as well as a copy of your driver's license.

The websites for each is as follows:

Equifax	www.equifax.com
Experian	www.experian.com
Trans Union	www.transunion.com

Correcting Errors

Under the FCRA, both the credit reporting company and the information provider/data furnisher, who is the person, company or organization that provides information about you to a credit reporting company are responsible for correcting inaccurate or incomplete information in your report. To take advantage of all your rights under this law, contact the credit reporting company **and** the information provider.

Tell the credit reporting company—in writing—exactly what information you think is inaccurate. You can find sample language in the credit repair letters in *Color My Credit.* Make sure you include copies—not originals—of the documents supporting your position.

In addition to providing your complete name and address, your letter should clearly identify each item in the report you dispute. State the facts simply, explain why you dispute the information, and request that it be removed or corrected. You may want to enclose a copy of your report with the items in question circled. If you are using regular mail, send it by certified mail, return receipt requested, so you can document when the reporting service received your mail. Keep copies of your dispute letter and all enclosures or attachments. Make a copy of your driver's license to include, as well.

Credit reporting companies must investigate the items in question—normally within 30 days—unless they consider your claim frivolous. They must also forward the relevant data you provide about the inaccuracy to the organization that provided the information in dispute.

After the information provider receives notice of a dispute from the credit reporting company, it must investigate, review the relevant information, and report the results back to the credit reporting company so the information can be corrected, if appropriate.

When the investigation is complete, the credit reporting company must give you the results in writing, and provide a free copy of your report—if the dispute resulted in a change. This free report does not count as your annual free report. If an item is changed or deleted, the credit reporting company cannot put the disputed information back on your file unless the information provider verifies it is accurate and complete. The credit reporting company must also send you written notice that includes the name, address and phone number of the information provider.

If you ask, the credit reporting company must send notices of any corrections to anyone who received your report in the past six (6) months. You can have a corrected copy of your report sent to anyone who received a copy during the past two (2) years for employment purposes.

If an investigation does not resolve your dispute with the credit reporting company, you can ask that a statement of the dispute be included in your file and future reports. You can also ask the credit reporting company to provide your statement to anyone who received a copy of your report in the recent past. You can, however, expect to pay a fee for this service.

Information Provider Notification and Request

Tell the information provider—the person, company, or organization that provided information about you to a credit reporting company—in writing that you dispute the item on your report.

Include copies—not originals—of documents that support your position. If the provider listed an address on your credit report, send your letter to that address. If no address is listed, contact the provider and ask for the correct address to send your letter. If the information provider does not give you and address, you can send your letter to any business address for that provider.

If the provide continues to report the item you disputed to a credit reporting company, it is required to let the credit reporting company know about your dispute. If you are correct—and the information is found to be inaccurate or incomplete—the information provider must tell the credit reporting company to update or delete the item. If nothing changes after you provide your dispute, you can request the credit agencies to send you a method of verification so you can determine what the information provider/data furnisher supplied, to verify the account does belong to you and is being accurately reported.

The Skinny on Creditors and How they Report

Your credit file may not reflect all your credit accounts. Although most national department store and all-purpose bank credit card accounts will be included in your file, not all creditors supply information to credit reporting companies. Some local retailers, credit unions, travel, entertainment and gasoline card companies are among creditors who do not report.

When negative information in your credit report is accurate, only the passage of time can assure its removal.

A credit reporting company can report most accurate negative information for seven (7) years from the date of first delinquency; bankruptcy information can be reported for ten (10) years from the discharge date. Information about a unpaid judgment against you can be reported for seven (7) years, or until the statute of limitations runs out; whichever is longer.

There is no time limit on reporting:

- √ Criminal convictions
- √ Information reported in response to an application for a job that pays more than $75,000 annually.

√ Information reported in application for more than $150,000 worth of credit or life insurance.

INSIDER TIP: TTHERE IS A STANDARD METHOD FOR CALCULATING THE SEVEN-YEAR REPORTING PERIOD. GENERALLY, THE PERIOD RUNS FROM THE DATE THE LAST ACTION ON YOUR PART TAKES PLACE. IF A CREDITOR CHARGES OFF AN ACCOUNT, AND SELLS IT TO A COLLECTION AGENCY, THE DATE OF FIRST DELINQUENCY DOES NOT CHANGE—UNLESS YOU MAKE ANY PAYMENT WITH THE COLLECTION COMPANY.

Chapter 3
Common Delinquencies on Credit Reports

THERE IS LITTLE need for carrying a lot of shame around and prevent you from taking a deep dive into your credit report and doing all you can to improve your score. In fact, if you face the issue with courage, you might just find a lot of things that are no longer relevant to a seven-year look, and many that may no longer be accurate. We do, however have to take a look at the delinquencies remaining on your report and determine what, if anything, can/or should be done to mitigate their damage.

Found as Derogatory Accounts

- √ Collections
- √ Late Payments
- √ Charge-offs

Found under Public Records

- √ Bankruptcies
- √ Tax Liens (Paid and Unpaid)
- √ Judgments

Here is what you need to know about public records. They aren't reported to the three credit bureaus. They are public records. The three credit bureaus hire third party servicers to go out and check county public records to manually add these bad accounts on your credit report. There is a protocol for getting them removed. Without following these plans, you could lose your opportunity to have it removed.

INSIDER SECRET: JUST PAYING IT WON'T DROP IT OFF YOUR CREDIT REPORT AND SOMETIMES IT IS BETTER TO NOT HAVE IT UPDATED OR REMOVED.

When paying a negative account that is showing on your credit report, there is no way to make it a good account. The negative account has an obligation upon receiving payment to update the ***date*** on your credit report of last activity, which you know by now moves it *back* into the Score Circle. This makes it look like the bad activity just occurred therefore dropping your credit score.

Unless you negotiate with the bad account to have the account deleted completely and get it in writing, it might be best to just show proof to your lender/creditor that it has been paid and not actually have the account updated. If it is a public record, YOU must send in the documentation to show the debt was paid or released to make sure the information is updated. The bureaus pay people to go out and find the information, but it is highly doubtful they are going to pay someone to see that accounts are paid.

Chapter 4
Common Credit Report Errors and How to Dispute Them

From the errors of others, a wise man corrects his own.

~ **Publilius Syrus** (85 BC-43 BC)
Roman Author.

DID YOU KNOW every person living in America who has any credit reported within the past 6 months could have 70+ credit scores, depending on the model, the agency, and the credit score type?

Did you know... the Federal Trade Commission (FTC) recently reported a significant number of consumers had errors on their report and 26% had errors that were likely to impact their ability to secure credit at a favorable rate? What exactly does this mean for you... just that you are best to take advantage of the Fair Credit Reporting Act to secure your annual free copy, and to make sure you are making your request for the Annual Credit Report and not be taken in by other sites leading you to believe you must pay them a fee for the service.

The Most Common Credit Report Errors

OBVIOUSLY THERE ARE myriad types of errors that can negatively impact the color credit report you are seeking to color, but the following list should put up red flag alerts for you.

> ***Accounts closed by lender:*** Although it is not good advice to close accounts, if you have, you will want to make sure the account has not been listed in error as "closed by grantor."
>
> ***Bad debt exceeding seven years:*** Credit reporting companies are required to remove all bad debt older than seven years, and all debts discharged in a bankruptcy.
>
> ***Duplicate accounts:*** Sometimes accounts are reported more than once. That makes it look like you have more open credit and higher debt.
>
> ***Former spouse obligations:*** This is a bit of advance planning relative to a potential divorce... remove your name from any joint accounts to ensure you are not liable for any future debt a spouse may incur. Check your report following the divorce to ensure the request for removal from the account was done.
>
> ***Incorrect personal information:*** The spelling of your name, with the inclusion of your middle name if you normally use it to sign legal documents. It is not infrequently that reports reflect the information for persons with a similar name. Given the high incident of identity theft, it is wise to review all addresses,

employment information, and Social Security number(s) evident on your report.

How to Correct Credit Report Errors

- √ Once you are aware of an error on your report, understand it will require a unique blend of patience and effort to correct them. The following is a quick checklist of the steps you must take to color inside the credit report boundary lines.
- √ Communicate only in writing. *Although the primary companies do provide online* correction capabilities, the expert advice is to mail certified letters and keep copies to document unresolved disputes.
- √ Clearly explain what you believe the error is, include copies of documents that support your claim, a copy of the report with the error highlighted, and ask specifically for the removal of the error.
- √ If you have the contact information, send a copy of your letter and supporting documents to the entity reporting the error and ask them to make the correction to their records.
- √ *Write one letter per error.* If you find multiple errors, address each one in a separate

Section III

Buying A Home

MOST AMERICANS WANT to buy a home. Some address the biological need; based on a desire to next. Economic conditions... national issues... global disturbances... little seems to still the desire. Thomas Jefferson had the right perspective, "A right to property is founded in our natural wants."

A devastating housing and mortgage crash did not impact the desire, and although it resulted in millions of foreclosed homes and trillions of dollars of lost equity, collectively we have not given up the idea that buying a home colors the picture of our economic dream.

Waiting Periods

AS A MORTGAGE banker with a long history in the industry, it has almost become second nature for em to set aside buyer's fears about buying a home—with bad credit. The color of your report mad indeed impact the rates and loan programs available to you, but just because your credit is not stellar or you have filed bankruptcy, you always have the option to stand back, remain committed to your desire for home ownership, and work to make it happen… on your terms.

There are, however, certain periods of time which much lapse between certain events, and applying for a loan. We will look at the most common: foreclosures and bankruptcy.

Although the period between bankruptcy filings is about 7 years, the negative impact for your credit report is 10 years. Additionally, to better posture a mortgage with better conforming loan rates, that waiting period is four years following the filing of a bankruptcy or short sale.

If you plan an FHA loan, with which you can qualify with as little as 3.5% down, you will be required to wait 2 full years after a foreclosure, and 3 after a short sale. You may read some guidelines that state one year is the waiting period after a qualifying short sale, however, most lenders reject them.

Be cautious of the hard-money lenders who will entice you with loans just six months after filing bankruptcy or a foreclosure, but may a require as much as 35% down, with very unfavorable rates and loan terms.

Improve Conforming Loan Qualifications.

Don't walk away from the opportunity to purchase a home with bad credit just because someone has told you it's not possible! The whole purpose of working through the Color My Credit Method is to take the steps necessary to improve those scores over a period of time much smaller than you probably think and also improve your opportunity for a larger mortgage, less down payment, and better loan products and rates. The following steps can also expedite the process—providing you complete them as part of the overall Color My Credit program.

Credit Cards

Work to obtain a major credit card. If your actions follow the discharge of a bankruptcy, immediately apply for two secured credit cards and begin the financial habit of buying something for $10 or $20 each month and paying it off when the bill comes. Never spend more than that. Never use them as income or cash. They cannot buy a better life. You must drown out the bad with good and the further you get away from the discharged bankruptcy and re-establish a few pieces of credit, you will begin to reap the rewards of your credit score improving and keeping them high for the rest of you life.

These insider secrets also play a significant part in improving the boundaries you can set for better credit scores:

- √ Maintain steady employment and earn a regular salary or wage for one or two years.
- √ Show steady employment on the job for one to two years.
- √ Regularly add to a savings account for a down payment of at least 10% of the purchase price you feel you can afford.
- √ Avoid late payments at all costs; continue to pay all bills on time.

How FICO Scores Affect Interest Rates

If you spend time checking out the correlation between FICO scores and interest rates, you will discover the overall impact a low credit score, whether based on accurate or inaccurate information, could have on your ability to build wealth in your lifetime. For example, I recently had a Veteran looking to purchase a home and his credit score was a 639. By paying one credit card down by $40, he was able to raise the credit score up to a 645 and it dropped his interest rate. The payment ended up being $71 less a month, which made a huge impact on his ability to put money away for his retirement.

The interest rates are impacted by FICO scores—up to a 760 FICO score in most cases. The interest rate is typically then higher for scores between 759-740, 739-720, 719-700, 699-680... and so on.

One point in your credit score could make a difference in your interest rate and more importantly, if you are buying a home and putting less than 20% down, your credit score will have the same affect on the price you pay for the mortgage insurance. The difference could be hundreds of dollars a month for you in the monthly payment.

When you are ready to obtain a home insurance policy, your credit score will likely have a big impact on the price you pay for the home and auto insurance policies.

Never before has your credit score affected the price you pay so drastically—in order to obtain the big ticket items most people need to survive and function in life, like housing and transportation.

Section IV

Identity Theft
Protect Yourself

Unlike a drop of water, which loses its identity when it joins the ocean, man does not lose his being in the society in which he lives.
Man's life is independent. He is born not for the development of the society alone, but for the development of his self.

~ **B. R. Ambedkar** (1891-1956)
Indian Author and Politician.

Basic Fraud Services

NO ONE IS ever fully protected from identity theft; many people are not even aware they have been impacted until years later, when for one reason or another they pull a credit report. It is most unfortunate we now live with the combination of technology and culture that leaves us in a constant state of worry about data breaches and identity theft. Of course, whenever there is a problem, myriad business models pop up to provide the solution. Before you decide to enroll with any fraud service, complete your due diligence, weigh the costs and benefits of what is offered, If you're concerned about data breaches or identity theft, you may be considering signing up for identity theft protection services. Before you enroll, it's important to weigh the costs and benefits of various types of services, and—in essence—protect yourself from the protection!

Programs like *Color My Credit* can assist you to modify the damage once you are made aware of the situation; it can also serve to develop the kind of awareness and resources necessary to prevent the trauma and drama of being a victim of identity theft. Your first, best step is to review the IdentityTheft.gov website and familiarize yourself with its recovery plans and step-by-step guidance to help identity theft victims recover.

What are identity theft protection services?

Perhaps you want more clarity about my reference to identity theft protection services, but the number one myth I want to bust is that companies promising you identity theft protection should be required to disclose they are merely monitoring and recovery services. The reality remains... no service can totally protect you from becoming a victim of identity theft. What they can offer is to monitor your account and watch for signs you may be a victim. Most of them also help you best manage the fallout if identity theft occurs.

Monitoring Services

In your search you will see two types of monitoring services—credit and identity. Credit monitoring tracts all activity on your credit reports at one, two, or all three of the well-known bureaus: Equifax, Experian, and Transunion. Most people willingly pay for these services so the early alert will be more impactful in resolving problems before they get out of hand. The services offering credit monitoring will alert you when:

- √ Inquiries into your credit history.
- √ New loan or credit card accounts opened in your name.
- √ Creditor or debt collector notes your payment is late.

√ Public records show you've filed for bankruptcy or there is a legal judgment against you

√ Changes in credit limits.

√ Changes to personal information: name, address, or phone number.

Please remember credit monitoring is only used to warn you about unusual activity on your credit report. In fact, many types of identity theft never appear there. If, for example, your information is used to make bank withdrawals, file fraudulent tax returns or collect refunds—that information will not come from a credit monitoring service.

If you feel the comfort and efficiencies of using such a service, ask the following questions as part of your due diligence in selecting a reputable firm.

√ Which credit reporting agencies do you monitor?

√ How often do you monitor the reports?

√ What access will I have to my credit reports?

√ Which of the bureaus will I be able to review, how frequently can I review them, and will I be charged each time I review a report?

√ Do you include other services, such as access to my credit score?

The alerts will be created when there is any change to your personal information, including but not limited to bank account information, Social Security, driver's license, passport, or medical ID number. The monitoring is intended to pick up on how our information is used in ways that generally don't show up on your credit report, and will red flag:

- √ Request for change of address.
- √ Arrest, or other court records.
- √ Request for new utility, cable, or wireless services.
- √ Payday loan applications and/or check cashing requests.
- √ Changes in social media or other websites that identity thieves use to trade stolen information.

The effectiveness of these services is service and relationship they have with large national databases, but there are limitations to what they can access. Unfortunately, the nature of this restricted information is the core of what you really need the alerts for: tax or government benefits fraud; Medicare, Medicaid, welfare, and Social Security.

Identity recovery services

Identity recovery services have become big business, and stemmed to help victims regain control of their good name and finances after identity theft occurs. The services basically cover trained counselors or case managers who walk victims through the process of addressing identity theft problems. The services may include writing letters to creditors and debt collectors, placing a freeze on credit reports to prevent an identity thief from opening new accounts in your name, or guide you through reviewing myriad documents.

Identity theft insurance

One other layer of protection from identity theft is an specific insurance product offered by major identity theft protection services. The insurance is designed to cover only out-of-pocket expenses directly associated with reclaiming your identity; expenses typically limited to things like postage, copying, and notary costs. The policy generally doesn't reimburse you for any stolen money or financial loss resulting from the theft, although a limited few do include lost wages or legal fees. Most policies come with deductibles, limitations and exclusions.

As you have already experienced, at the end of the day, Color My Credit programs are more intrinsically designed to teach you how to monitor your credit reports with the free option available to you each year. The added word of wisdom is to review statements for credit cards, bank, and other brokerage and retirement accounts on a monthly basis. Another growing area of fraud you need to monitor is found on the explanation of benefits (EOB) statements you get from your health insurance providers. Sometimes these mistakes are little more than human error; however, if you see treatments you never received, immediately tell your insurer and medical providers.

Did you know... if you want to totally block identity thieves from opening new accounts in your name you can place a security freeze on credit files with the three major bureaus. This freeze effectively blocks anyone from accessing your reports without you first giving permission. The downside is if you need to provide that permission, it can take several days to "unlock" your file, as well as a fee that can range from $5 to $10 per event.

An action that does not come with a cost is to place a free, initial 90-day fraud alert with the bureaus if you believe you are an identity theft victim or, in the case you lost your wallet or received a data breach notice. Potential creditors and lenders are then required to contact you directly and verify your identity before opening new accounts in your name.

Electronic Signatures

BEFORE WE MOVE onto another topic, let's stare technology in the face and make sure we are coloring within the boundaries of lowering our risk. It is unfortunate we live in a society where each time you put something on the internet, the risk of it falling into the wrong hands is huge. Not everyone plays by the rules, and even with all the security options, it is extremely easy to have your data breached.

The risk is increased each time you upload sensitive information on your servers. Granted, the flexibility we need for work makes it necessary to retain certain information on cloud servers. We tend to believe there are more advantages than risks when using online applications and the risk does deter us from using them. The caveat is to do everything possible; to take the precautions available to protect yourself from possible data breach and identity theft.

There is definitely merit to the Internet's global system; a wonderful and frightening privilege that connects us and opens the risk to identity theft. Hackers are beyond brilliant is their evil; most things most of us could never fathom. The threat to our identity is a 24-7 concern… most Americans between the ages 18-44 have access to their phones literally 24 hours a day. We no longer use landlines, we shop and pay our bills on these handy devices, and with the widely accepted practice of signature tools, even executing legal documents no longer has to be done in person. Let's look at the steps you might want to consider to protect your digital signature.

- √ Do not use a digital signature software until you are certain there are authentication measures completed before a signer executes the document.
- √ Inquire whether documents are encrypted and protected when placed on a cloud-based server—and what security measures are employed to ensure information held there will remain tamper free.
- √ Determine whether the software being used has an alarm system. Since there is such a large market for the product, security can vary significantly from vendor to vendor.
- √ Did you know… one of the questions you might put forth is to discover whether digital shredding is used. We all know when files are deleted they are not gone… they are simply hidden and forgotten. Digital shredding is the level of protection you want to ensure

is being uses; deleted files are overwritten a sufficient number of times the original information can no longer be viewed.

√ Did you also know… every person who wants to use digital signatures has to apply for a digital certificate from a certifying authority. This certificate is strictly monitored by third-party services and not given to just anyone. It requires a verification process to ensure you are who you say you are. A private key is provided for every digital signature used—to later validate the signature and ensure to tampering occurred after the document was signed. The authentication process makes it impossible for anyone to use your signature or open your documents.

Section V

Credit Rescoring and Buying Power

RESTORING YOUR CREDIT is the underlying focus of *Color My Credit,* however, given the possibility any certain number of readers might glance in the table of contents and head directly for the absolute skinny on improving their score... I wanted to make that possible. I understand how a bad credit score looms over you like a dark cloud. I understand the desire to buy a home, get a student loan, secure insurance, or apply for a next-level career position only to be severely bruised emotionally when nothing can happen—bad credit is a brick wall separating you. *Color My Credit* is filled with myriad options to improve your score and lift the dark cloud... my hope is you will read this quick checklist and decide to take advantage of the remainder of the tools, tips, techniques, and the fun and engaging exercises found throughout the pages. But, first things first... read on!

Step 1: Know what you're dealing with.

Bad credit and harassing creditors can drain the best from just about anyone... to the point where the common response is to toss bills aside and ignore your debt problems. I can't sugar-coat this issue; the first—and most important—step is to step up to the plate and face the facts. The journey to restored credit begins with the first step of requesting a copy of your free annual credit report from the FTC authorized website and know what you have to deal with. I encourage you to use the assessment tools in **Color My Credit** as a guide.

AnnualCreditReport.com

Step 2: Know how much available credit you use.

You will hear the term, credit utilization ratio. It is one of the factors used to determine your FICO score. List each open line of credit and make note of the current credit limit on each. To calculate this number, you're your current card balance(s) and divide by the total credit limit, then multiply that number by 100. For example, if you owe $2,000 on a card with a $10,000 limit, your credit utilization ratio is 20%.

Use these ratios to your benefit to assuage negative impact on your score. You might consider setting a goal to have a 25% utilization ratio on each credit line in your name. You might also want to focus on being more aggressive with paying down the card that has the highest utilization ratio first.

Step 3: Add a Secured Credit Card.

You may think I am giving poor advice here, but listen on... it is a given that past mistakes make it difficult to build a positive credit history when you can't secure a regular credit card. There is a phrase about doing the best you can with what you currently have available to you; in this case, a secured card might just be all that is available. Secured cards allow you to deposit a small amount of money as a form of collateral to the lender. Use the card and make regular, on-time payments to reestablish positive credit. Note: Do not select a company that does not report to each of the major credit bureaus.

Step 4: Stay on top of your payments.

If you review other parts of Color My Credit, you will see multiple references to the importance of payment history on your credit score—do whatever it takes to manage this new opportunity to build a healthy, positive credit history. Commit to missing no payments on existing or new debt. Greater wisdom would have you budget amounts specifically for debt repayment each month.

You will also see references in other sections of *Color My Credit* to keep your credit line open if at all possible even after you have paid the debt in full. It will demonstrate longer-term responsible use of available credit.

Step 5: Expand your options.

Trust me, if you stay on the path, you will come to a point where you will have a handle on spending habits, and will have boosted those scores. You will now have the privilege of switching from the secured credit card and might even be able to qualify for a student or vehicle loan if you need them. This diversification of credit types reflects a growing ability to manage your credit and will further improve your scores.

Proceed with caution and open the additional lines only as you need them, and never all at the same time. Too many new credit inquiries in a short time frame can reverse all the work you did to restore your credit.

I trust you will have benefited from the previous steps. They are a good place to start. There is more help for you throughout Color My Credit, but if I do, indeed, have this one opportunity to deliver a message to you, it would be this...

Restoring your credit takes time and dedication.

Since most credit reports cover the past seven years, you can understand why can take a long time to make improvements to your score. There are some really great insider tips in Color My Credit that can expedite the process; that process can only begin by taking action. Request your credit reports today and if you do nothing else that is discussed in *Color My Credit*, you will be on your way to saying no to bad credit, and yes to living your goals and dreams.

Section VI

Recent Changes and The Future of Credit Reporting

They always say time changes things, but you actually have to change them yourself.

~ **Andy Warhol** (1928-1987)
American Artist.

THE ONE CONSTANT in life will always be change. How do we address that in the greater scope of trying to best manage credit? Primarily, the answer to that is to monitor what transpires in the industry, either by your own methods or by staying connected with your favorite "credit guru!"

What I can share with you at the time of going to print with *Color My Credit* is the changes that were on board in June, 2016. As we have discovered on this credit restoration journey, the current reporting system is not always friendly to consumers. The Consumer Financial Protection Board (CFPB) frequently shares industry complaints regularly received, and sometimes, I think they listen to you! The long, often immobilizing process to get egregious errors removed from your records are covered in a proposed bill, the Comprehensive Consumer Credit Reporting Reform Act.

What changes are being proposed?

The bill, introduced on May 19 proposes quite a number of changes to the credit reporting and scoring process; many of which will impact homebuyers and their resulting mortgages. Fortunately, we can look to changes that will affect all U.S. citizens with a credit history, including the following important aspects of the bill:

Rapid removal of negative items.

The bill will mandate maximum time limits on responses for removal, as well as a maximum amount of time remaining on your report reduced to four years. If the bill passes, bankruptcies, which currently remain up to 10 years, would be removed after 7 years.

Negative information notification.

Wow! What will it be like; the first time a creditor reports negative information, to a credit bureau, it would be legally required to notify you. The value here, as I see it, is victims of identity theft to catch accounts opened in their names sooner rather than later.

Transparent dispute and reporting.

Did you know... one of the chief complaints people have it the difficult of disputing errors, and holding the bureaus a little more accountable for the accuracy on your reports.,

Offering free annual credit scores.

As we have discussed, you are currently entitled to a free annual report; the new bill will entitle you to the same annual privilege of an annual score as well.

Standardized scoring model.

Some content the FICO model is outdated; factors for new credit scores will include minimizing the impact of disputed or paid off medical accounts, and incorporating data demonstrating good credit habits, such as rental payments which are now not considered.

How long must we wait?

I guess we have to be patient! The introduction of the bill is relatively new and many are altered before they become law so... we have to wait out the storm and be happy for whatever extra representation we, as consumers, gain in the process. Once you connect with Color My Credit... you can rest assured you will be among the first to be alerted to credit reporting and scoring changes.

Section VII

Common Credit Questions

Take the attitude of a student, never be too big to ask questions, never know too much to learn something new.

~ **Og Mandino** (1923-1996)
American Author.

THERE IS NEVER a way for me to know what someone else doesn't know! The questions come at me from fear of the unknown, personal experiences that shatter lives, and from deep in the heart. It is safe to say I can respond to virtually any question, and to start you on the road to being ok with asking the questions that will help you remove the blocks that prevent you from having the credit score you deserve, I am posting a few here. These are probably the more common questions I have been asked, but remember—there is no dumb question—ever!

I have an old mortgage on my credit report that I know has been paid. If I request an update to correct that information, will it help my credit score?

Most likely the old mortgage is not affecting your score. Balances that most impact your numbers are balances on revolving debt. Check the credit card balances that are charged—up to or close to their limit.

Will it help me to show a collection account paid off?

If the collection account is over 12 months old, there is actually a chance it is having a negative effect at the onset. The bureaus look at this as this kind of a correction as bringing derogatory information to a current date. If the collection account is reporting in the last 12 months, there is more of a chance of the modification having a positive affect, thought it will probably not be a dramatic increase.

Will showing a judgment or lien satisfied/released help my score?

Again, if the judgment is over 12 months old, there is a chance it is being considered negatively on your score—for the same reasons as in the previous question.

There is a collection agency reporting on the credit report and I have a letter from the original creditor showing it paid. How will that impact my score?

The bureaus will not accept your letter. The proof must be from the company that is actually reporting to the bureaus. In this case, it would be from the collection agency. If the original creditor is also reporting on a separate line, you must obtain letters from both.

What can I do about my bankruptcy?

As a general rule, I discourage clients from requesting updates on Bankruptcies, especially if it was discharged over 12 months ago. By showing charge-offs/collections included in a bankruptcy again, the bureaus look at the action as bringing derogatory information to a current date, and it could actually have a negative impact on your report.

Someone advised me to close out all the old credit cards showing up on my credit report. If I do this, will it improve my score?

No! And in most cases, it will actually lower the very score you are trying to improve You see, closing old, unused credit cards also removes their history and length of history accounts for 15% of your credit score.

What about charges for credit repair?

The process I use is rapid rescore—not credit repair. The bureaus are in a rather precarious position... managing data for millions of creditors. They are wise to position themselves to avoid being accused of a conflict of interest, profiteering from errors, or accusations of ulterior motives for errors appearing on consumer reports. They provide rapid rescore to mortgage lenders to update credit information and scores in 3-5 days versus waiting 30 days or more for the information to be updated. It is a fee mortgage lenders must absorb and cannot be passed on to the consumer, therefore many banks don't allow loan officers to use it.

Exactly how do I determine what might improve my score?

Ordering a credit report and sitting down and really taking a deep dive into what is reflected there is your first, best step! The score factor is what you want to look at first; they are in order of importance. The top two listed are always what has the most impact Also, I use a Credit Analyzer and a What If simulator to help my clients determine the best course of action to take to improve scores. Don't try to do it all at once.

After you have colored your report, you should have one to 4 pages on average of accounts to tackle… .not a 150 page credit report to get lost in.

A lot of the information on my report is really old, I don't know if I have the documentation the bureaus might ask for. What documents will they accept and what would be considered as not acceptable?

Let's look at the first question: What documentation is acceptable? For a lender to do a rapid rescore, this is what is needed:

To show a balance paid down, we need a copy of a mailed statement, or an online snapshot that shows the new balance once the account has been paid down.

If it is an online snapshot, the document must show the company log, at least the last four digits of the account number, and reflect what the new/current balance it.

An online snapshot of a new balance will work for every credit card company except American Express or FNB.

Now, for the documents that are not acceptable; the list is long! Bureaus will not accept divorce decrees, HUDS, settlement statements, copies of money orders, department store receipts, Universal Data Forms, or online snapshots for credit cards that only show a payment was made, but does not reflect the new balance. The bureaus will also not accept any document over 30 days old.

I have seen things on my credit report show a dispute remark I want removed. What is the process to do that?

In most cases, all you need to do is write a letter noting your dispute. Make sure the letter is typed, signed, dated and references the account name and number as it appears on your credit report. All you need to state is, "I am not disputing this account; please remove the dispute remark."

If the remark on the report reads "reinvestigation in progress" it is not possible to complete a rescore to have it removed. This notation is reported only by Equifax and the company will not allow for the removal of the remark.

The only way to have it removed is to contact the Office of Consumer Affairs at Equifax… advise them you are not disputing the account, and wish to withdraw the dispute and have the remark removed.

Section VIII

Credit Tips to Live By

When you encourage others, you in the process are encouraged because you're making a commitment and difference in that person's life. Encouragement really does make a difference.

~ **Zig Ziglar** (1926-2012)
American author and motivational speaker.

Do This and More

MUCH OF THIS book has been about restoring your credit. *Color My Credit* would not possibly be complete without sharing how to continue to keep it that way. A life successful at many levels requires developing and maintain good habits; it also demands us to be fully aware of what we need to do, use the tools that help us do what we must, and hold a commitment to a long-term goal. I encourage you to continue this journey with me...

Annual Credit Report Review

Check your report for accuracy once a year for free by going to www.annualcreditreport.com.

Dispute anything that is an error directly with the three credit bureaus by going to the websites of Transunion, Experian, and Equifax.

If you plan on buying a home in the future, make sure you work with a lender who can build a specific game plan for you to raise your mortgage score the fastest to get you the most favorable interest rates and insurance premiums.

Derogatory credit and collections are only supposed to stay on your credit for 7 years from the date of first delinquency or the first time your payment started the road to delinquency. If it has been longer that, **you** need to dispute it and get it removed. If the information is missing or any part of it is inaccurate, you need to dispute it and get it removed.

Manage your credit limits.

If your credit cards are maxed out, call your credit card company and request for a credit line increase **or** pay the balance down below 20% of the limit with an installment loan. Banks that offer installment loans include Lending Club, Prosper, Springleaf, and Loanme. Thirty percent of your credit score is based on the ratio of your credit card limit versus the balance the lender reports. Installment loans are not taken into account in the limit versus balance ratio so essentially just transferring your credit card debt to one of these installment loans could raise your credit score considerably without you having to immediately reduce the amount currently owed on your cards.

Remember to keep the credit cards open though and begin your do- over relationship with them. Drop the last number on the limit for the credit card and that is the true limit for you. If it is a $200 limit, your true limit is $20 and is the amount you should consistently spend and pay off on auto-pay when the bill arrives. Keep it simple. Never use your credit cards as cash or income again.

Review open credit card accounts.

Do you have an open credit card you forgot you opened back in the day but it is still active? Call the company to request a new card and make a small purchase. That's right... go buy something. If you have not used the account in more than 24 months it is likely not being factored into your current credit score as an open account... and length of time is 15% of your credit score analysis. I have personally seen clients who have increased their score 30 points just by making a $30 purchase at JC Penny's or Victoria's Secret after realizing they **still** had an open account they had not used in a very long time.

Don't rush to pay off installment loans.

Don't rush to pay off your installment loans (car loan, furniture, medical) or closed accounts. Every month you make a payment maintains a good score; however, paying it off, the account automatically closes and to the scoring model it looks like you have a lot less credit available to you.

Remember if your lease is up and you are going in for a new lease, your credit will likely take a dip because one account will close and a brand new inquiry and account will show. This calls for you to be strategic with your timing when considering a car right before a home purchase where the dip in your score could cost you thousands in the mortgage rate over the life of the loan.

Rely on auto-payments.

Set anything you can up on auto payments through your bank account. If you set it up through a debit card, you must watch that the payment still goes through each month. There are increasing reports of payments showing up missed due to a debit card malfunction and the borrower being on auto-pilot in believing it is paid.

If you have a 30-day late showing on your credit report in the last 30 days, the best use of your time would be to call the creditor and request a "goodwill removal." Tell them you had never been late before and it is greatly affecting your credit. Request something in writing stating they will remove the 30-day late. If they say no, ask if you make the next three payments on time would they agree to remove the 30-day late then? If they say no, call back and try again. Be persistent. It is worth your time getting late payments removed. Nothing will help your score more than removing lates that have occurred in the last 24 months and you are able to get the creditor to remove them. Put on your game face! Make it happen!

When you pay makes a big difference.

Do you use your credit cards for business but pay them off in full each month? When are you making your payments on credit cards? You might be making your payment in full every month but you make the payment on the 9th and the creditor reports to the credit bureaus on the 8th of every month.

Regardless of the due date, the day that specific creditor reports to the bureaus is the amount that will show on the credit report for 30-45 days or more, depending on how often that creditor reports to the bureaus. Some creditors don't report to all three bureaus which is often why you see a variation in the three scores. Make sure to call your creditors and ask them **who** they report to each month and what **day they report** each month—then mark it in your calendar or phone to remind you so you can pay the balance down before they report. This one small step could improve your score 100 points or more. Check your credit card balance when it comes in the mail—that is typically the amount that has been reported to the credit bureau, not the amount you pay.

Review derogatory and collection accounts.

If a derogatory account or collection is reporting on your credit report, review the **date last updated** or **date last reported**. If it is more than 24 months ago, it is not being factored into the score. Any activity, even paying it off, could drop your score drastically unless you get them to agree to delete it if you pay it. You can never make a collection become good on your credit report unless it is removed—paying it **does not remove** it. If the debt **does fall within the last 24 months** and the creditor won't delete it no matter what, you are better off negotiating a settlement with the collection company and getting a letter in writing showing paid in full.

Keep all correspondence so you have proof of the settlements and immediately send a copy to the three credit bureaus. No one is working for you. If you want the job done right, do it yourself or ask for help and be willing to learn.

Know what credit score you are looking at.

There are over 50 different models/scores for each of the credit bureaus depending on the type of credit you are applying for. Credit Karma and other free sites use Vantage Scores, which is FICO's competition created by the three bureaus (Transunion, Experian and Equifax) but less than 3% of all creditors use Vantage Score. These services have completely different criteria for what makes up a score but the score range is similar to FICO so it can appear to be a FICO score.

Mortgage companies **only use FICO scores** and only use specific models that consumers can't access as of yet. If you want to improve your score for a mortgage, you have to work with a lender who knows how to build a plan to improve your mortgage score.

Add authorized users.

One quick and easy way to get credit if you have none or your spouse or child is trying to build/rebuild credit is to add them as an authorized user to your credit card. You just have to contact the creditor and request to add them. At any time they can be removed and they don't need to receive a card to use. The user will get "credit" for your history on their score, as it will affect the length of history and payment history for the spouse or child who is lacking those things. Don't worry... whatever they have on their own report is not contagious.

Credit score look-back period.

Many people think a credit report is based on your life history of making payments and that is just not true. Your credit scores are mostly affected by the last 24 months of reported information. Just by starting today, no matter where your scores are, obtaining a couple of secured credit cards and consistently applying the financial habit of buying something for $10-$20 each month and paying it off, you could be on your way to better credit and be on your way to purchasing a home, car or insurance policy for considerably less... so you can then apply that savings to building a retirement and legacy.

Check www.colormycredit.com to stay educated on the latest tips and tricks and never forget... you are smarter than you think!

Section IX

ALISA OFFERS SOLUTIONS

We are at the very beginning of time for the human race. It is not unreasonable that we grapple with problems. But there are tens of thousands of years in the future. Our responsibility is to do what we can, learn what we can, improve the solutions, and pass them on.

~ **Richard P. Feynman** (1916-1988)
American Physicist

Color My Credit is not the only solution Alisa offers… you may also be interested in the following:

ILLUMI-NATION

ALISA'S PASSION SHINES all over this offering! She brings light to seven key financial areas that are crucial to building a financial legacy, each of which comes with complicated financial documents that need clear explanation and navigation.

You will have the distinct opportunity to engage with a network of professionals in the areas of budgeting, credit, taxes, insurance, mortgage and real estate, and retirement and estate planning—professionals who are committed to bringing value to their clients and community and considered natural educators at heart. Members of Illumination Professionals share their expertise, insider tips and tricks as they educate other professionals in related fields to illuminate the key areas of financial potential.

Never invest in any idea that cannot be illustrated/illuminated with a crayon!

Reminded once again of Robert Fulghum's quote... what if we did have his Crayola bomb? "It would explode high in the air—explode softly—and send thousands, millions, of little parachutes into the air. Floating down to earth—boxes of Crayola's."

Ah! I just love it!

ALISA SAYS…

For reading *Color My Credit.* We trust you have

enjoyed

each rich possibility for… a real look into the world of credit and how it colors your lives.

Walking through the financial maze can be challenging for everyone, but the tips and tools in *Color My Credit* allow you and your family to clearly identify how to find success in the credit game so you can focus on a successful transformation of where your credit is today–and where you would prefer it to be.

Color My Credit is designed to provide the roadmap to successful financial performance by laying out the boundaries and allowing you to color within the lines. And that is that! That is how you color··· your credit! You will gain knowledge to make the right moves for your financial present and future, and confidence to know you are performing at peak levels in the credit game

Thank you in advance for taking the time to post a review for the book on Amazon; many readers will not take that step to purchase and read… until they know someone else has led the way.

If you enjoyed reading *Color My Credit* I would appreciate it if you would help others enjoy the book, too.

LEND IT. This book is lending enabled, so please feel free to share with a friend.

RECOMMEND IT. Please help other readers find the book by recommending it to readers' groups, discussion boards, Goodreads, etc.

REVIEW IT. Please tell others why you liked this book by reviewing it on the site where you purchased it, on your favorite book site, or your own blog.

EMAIL ME. I'd love to hear from you.

colormycredit@gmail.com

CALL us at : 484-40-CREDIT

VISIT at www.colormycredit.com

OTHER BOOKS BY ALISA GLUTZ

The books that help you most are those which make you think most! The hardest way of learning is that of easy reading; but a great book that comes from a great thinker is a ship of thought, deep freighted with truth and beauty.

~ **Pablo Neruda** (1904-1973)
Chilean writer.

A **PROLIFIC WRITER**, Alisa Glutz has how you choose to color your world covered! Soon to be released you will discover a world that includes many smaller publications that can help you find the clarity you need - when you need it - and starts with asking the right questions... not searching for the right answers.

In each book you can count on engaging in the author's ***Color My***™ method to approach key financial areas from a child-like perspective. Her ultimate intention is to:

√ **Simplify complex subjects.**

√ **Use color to enhance understanding.**

√ **Incorporate play into education.**

√ **Encouraging questions... keeping readers alive with wonder.**

√ **Use visual aids to simplify and illuminate complicated and overwhelming financial areas, which are key to building a financial legacy.**

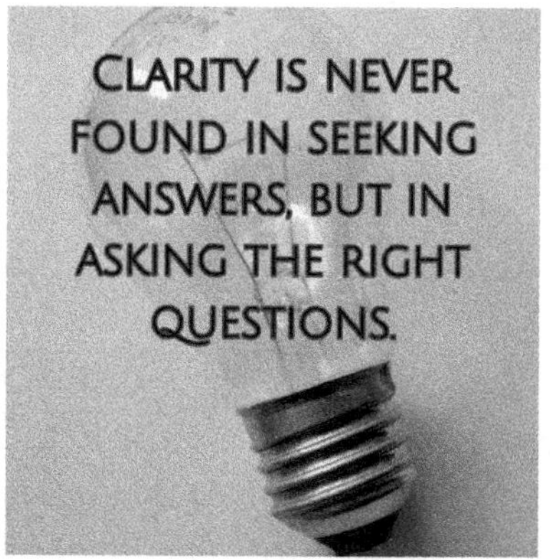

Color My...

Budget – answers simple questions such as:

- √ Why do I want or need to budget?
  - √ How much do I want/need to save?
  - √ How much time will it take me?
- √ Credit – answers important questions, like:
- √ Where can I get a report?
- √ Why do I even care?
- √ What is actually reflected on my report?
- √ How do I fix it?
- √ Taxes – *a rather complex* series of questions you might want answered:
- √ Where do my taxes go?

- √ When do I have to pay them?
- √ What happens if I don't?
- √ How to I keep more of my money?

Insurance - questions might include issues you may never have even considered:

- √ What exactly am I insuring?
- √ When does a policy normally renew?
- √ How much coverage do I really need?
- √ What types of coverage should I have?
- √ When should I file a claim vs. "eat the cost?"

Mortgage - this line of questioning covers one of the largest purchase items of your life, including:

- √ Why should I buy a home? Rent vs. Purchase
- √ What cost (hidden) am I going to incur?
- √ How do I get the best interest rate?
- √ When is it wise to refinance?

Retirement - questions about retirement are all too often put off being asked, almost until it is too late to act!

- √ How much do I need to retire?
- √ Where are the hidden money traps and risks in each possible investment product/vehicle?
- √ What are the best plans for me, and the lifestyle I want to have?

Legacy - these questions put your life in the open as you ask yourself what really matters... now and in the future:

- √ What do I want to leave to this world as a legacy of my time here?

- √ Who is important to me that I would want to know something critical?
- √ Do I actually need a will or a trust - or both?
- √ What can I do to best prepare my loved ones?

RESOURCES

My message to you all is of hope, courage and confidence. Let us mobilize all our resources in a systematic and organized way and tackle the grave issues that confront us with grim determination and discipline worthy of a great nation.

~ **Muhammad Ali Jinnah** (1876-1948)
Pakistani Politician

YOU ARE INVITED to continue the *Color My Credit* journey with me! Reading the book offered you enough wisdom, I trust, for you to begin taking charge of your credit and controlling how it impacts your future. This information was the 'head" stuff you must have to move forward... playing with me in the *Color My Credit* playground is the "heart" of making that task fun, fun, fun!

Pop on over to the playground at

http://colormycredit.com/color-my-credit-resources/ and enjoy the growing list of resources made available to you, my valued reader and partner in moving our communities to a better economic picture...

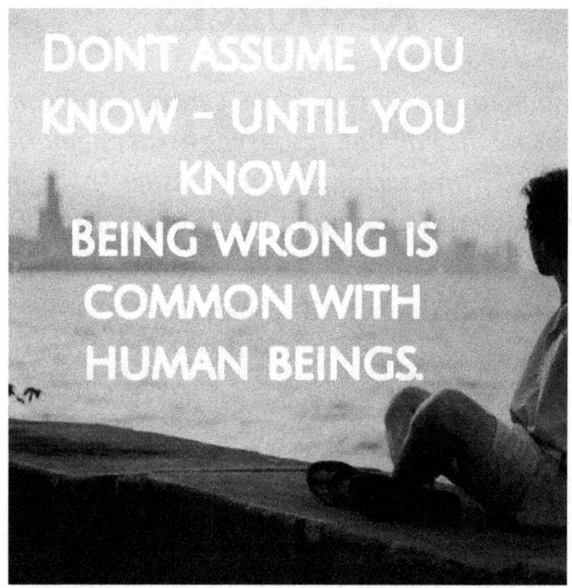

NOTES

CPSIA information can be obtained
at www.ICGtesting.com
Printed in the USA
LVHW081555210420
654191LV00009B/744

9 780692 783528